animal behavior

JOHN STIDWORTHY

PRENTICE HALL

New York   London   Toronto   Sydney   Tokyo   Singapore

ANIMAL BEHAVIOR

Managing Editor: Lionel Bender
Art Editor: Ben White
Text Editor: David Burn
Assistant Editor: Madeleine Samuel
Project Editor: Graham Bateman
Production: Clive Sparling

Media conversion and typesetting
Peter MacDonald and Partners and
Brian Blackmore

AN ANDROMEDA BOOK

Devised and produced by:
Andromeda Oxford Ltd
11–15 The Vineyard
Abingdon
Oxfordshire OX14 3PX
England

Prepared by Lionheart Books

Library of Congress Catalog Card
Number: 91-67000

ISBN 0-13-033390-5

Published in North America by:

Prentice Hall General Reference
15 Columbus Circle
New York, New York 10023

PRENTICE HALL and colophon are
registered trademarks of Simon &
Schuster, Inc.

Origination by Alpha Reprographics
Ltd,
Harefield, Middx, England
Manufactured in Singapore

10 9 8 7 6 5 4 3 2 1

First Prentice Hall Edition

CONTENTS

INTRODUCTION

Why do animals act the way they do? This book sets out to answer this question, and the process reveals how biologists – scientists who study living things – find out about the natural world and how they interpret the information they collect. We are interested in the way other animals behave because we hope that understanding them may help us to understand ourselves and for the practical contribution their study may make to human welfare and survival. Studying animal behavior is also important if we are to devise ways of protecting and conserving wildlife.

This book is divided into several sections. The first deals with the history of animal behavior studies and the various methods used. The next section, the largest, looks in turn at the major areas of behavior, including finding food and feeding, living in groups, aggression and defense, migration, communication and courtship. The third section deals with instinct, intelligence and learning. The last section deals with animals as builders, with sleep and other natural rhythms, and with culture in animals.

Each article in this book is devoted to a specific aspect of the subject. The text starts with a short scene-setting story that highlights one or two of the topics described in the article. It then continues with details of the most interesting aspects, illustrating the discussion with specific examples. It also covers conservation and people's relationships with their fellow animals and, where relevant, with plants.

Within the main text and photo captions in each article, the common or everyday names of animals and plants are used. For species illustrated in major artworks but not described elsewhere, the common and scientific (Latin) names of species are given in the caption accompanying the artwork. The index, which provides easy access to text and illustrations, is set out in alphabetical order of common names and of animal and plant groupings with the scientific names of species shown in parentheses.

A glossary provides definitions and short explanations of important technical terms used in the book. There is also a Further Reading list giving details of books for those who wish to take the subject further.

◄A school of snapper fish (*Lutjanus* species). Individuals within the group lessen their chances of predation by staying close to the center.

STUDYING BEHAVIOR

A man sits in a drafty hide, looking at the birds outside. But he is not a bird-spotter just hoping to see as many species as possible. He is interested in birds of just one kind. In front of the hide they are calling and courting one another. The man takes notes and records their voices. He recognizes individuals. He watches for hours at a time. He wants to know exactly what they do in the wild. He is studying bird behavior.

Humans have always been interested in the animals around them. For primitive people this was a necessity. They had to know which animals were good to hunt, and which might hunt them. It was also important for these early hunters to know what the animals did, as well as what they looked like, in order to outwit them. The various things that animals do are known collectively as behavior. Even today, knowledge of animal behavior is still important. With it we can manage farm animals better, and attempt to look after threatened or rare species. It may also help us to understand our own behavior.

FROM STORIES TO STUDIES

Although people have known something about animal behavior for thousands of years, their knowledge and understanding was very patchy. Some of it was merely unreliable folklore. For example, the Reverend Gilbert White – an English amateur naturalist who lived in the late 18th century – believed that swallows, which seemed to disappear after the summer, spent the winter hibernating in the mud at the bottom of ponds. We now know, of course, that they migrate to warmer regions. Yet White did make many careful observations and new discoveries, one of which was to recognize the difference between the chiffchaff and Willow warbler (see page 7). His idea about swallows may seem amusing now, but with the knowledge he had at the time he obviously thought it was quite reasonable. Remember also that he lived in an age when it was generally believed that animals had been created just as they are today. There was no reason to seek explanations for any of their behavior – it was just the way they had been made.

Since Englishman Charles Darwin put forward his ideas on evolution around the middle of the 19th century, however, there has been another way

▲ Bushmen in southern Africa carved these animal images in the rock many years ago. Knowing how animals behave is vital for such people, who depend on hunting them for food.

of looking at the things animals do. If the survival of a species depends on its adapting to its surroundings, then all aspects of the animal, its behavior as well as the way its body is made, must play a part. Long legs to carry an animal quickly away from danger are useless without an instinct that compels it to run when danger is near.

The realization that all behavior evolves just as physical characteristics do, made organized study possible.

Animal behaviorists
Three of the people who started the study of how animals behave in natural conditions. Konrad Lorenz (1903–89, left), an Austrian, is especially known for his work with geese, showing how young animals recognize their mother. The Dutchman Niko Tinbergen, born in 1907 (center), studied animal behavior in the wild on a range of creatures from insects to birds. Karl von Frisch (1886–1982, right), a German, worked on honeybees, which he showed could "talk" by means of dances. In 1972 all three of these ethologists received a Nobel Prize in recognition of their contribution to our understanding of behavior.

The complex activities of advanced animals, including ourselves, are so much more understandable when we regard them as developments of the simpler behavior that existed a long time ago. Until this approach was adopted, our knowledge of behavior was largely a jumble of descriptions and stories, some true, some wrong.

A NEW SCIENCE

In the 20th century the study of behavior has expanded into an important branch of biology. Within it there are two main disciplines. One of these, psychology, is concerned mainly with the behavior of people, but psychologists may also study other animals to discover rules of behavior common to all species, or to use them as "simplified" examples

Bird song

A Savannah sparrow (left) sings from a prominent perch. Birds sing not for pleasure (pleasant though their songs may be to us), but to convey information. This sparrow is "shouting" his ownership of the area round about. The warblers below can be told apart by their songs (shown as "sound pictures," right), although they look very similar. Songs may also be used to attract mates. In most birds only the males sing, but in a very few species females do so.

Willow warbler

A fluent song, lasting about 2 seconds and regularly repeated; a gentle series of descending notes.

Chiffchaff

A rather simple song, fixed on two notes, a high-pitched "chiff-chaff" or occasionally "zip-zap".

Wood warbler

Two distinct songs, the first a repeated single note, speeding up into a whistling trill, the second a mellow liquid "dee-ur".

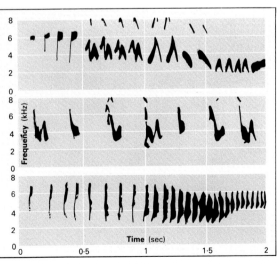

for human behavior. Such study takes place chiefly in the laboratory. The other main discipline is known as ethology. This is the study of animal behavior for its own sake, with emphasis on the animal's place in nature. Ethology is mainly concerned with the behavior of animals living freely in the wild, although sometimes they may be brought into the laboratory so that some aspect can be studied more closely.

QUESTIONS TO ANSWER

Niko Tinbergen, a 20th century Dutch animal behaviorist and one of the "founders" of ethology, has said that ethologists should strive to answer

Advanced behavior in primates

◄Orang-utans are good at learning. Sometimes they can work out puzzles by themselves, but do not always cooperate with human experimenters.

◄Some animals show their emotions through their facial expressions. This is especially noticeable in some of our close relations, as well as ourselves. Chimpanzees show a play face (1), begging for food (2), anger (3), intense fear (4), giving up (5), fear (6).

▼Facial signals in people. The shape of a baby's face (1) makes adults want to protect the child. Simple smile (2). Upper smile (3), made when saying hello. Broad smile (4), seen during laughing or play (5). Raising eyebrows (6) during greeting.

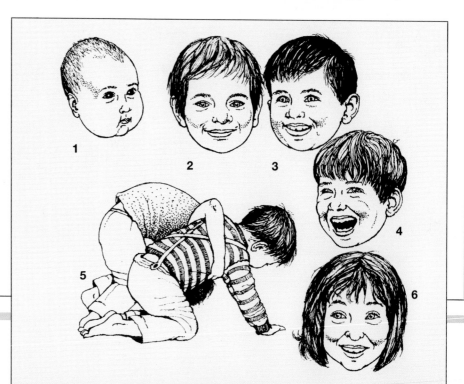

four different types of question. First, what is the immediate cause of a piece of behavior? For instance, what triggers fighting or courting in a mature male stickleback in the spring? Second, what function does the behavior serve? Animals rarely seem to be doing something "just for fun." Nearly always there is a reason for it. Third, how does the behavior develop in the individual? In many animals the behavior of the young is different from that of the adult. We would like to know what influences this change.

The fourth question is, how has the behavior altered with time or evolved. Perhaps such a question is not worth asking, because signs of behavior of animals long ago dead are extremely scarce. However, behavior is often very similar in species we know by other means to be close relations, and thus we may be able to infer "evolutionary stages" in behavior among living species.

WHAT IS IT ALL FOR?

There are two levels of answer to the question "What is the function of this behavior?" The first is an explanation of the immediate function. When a male hippopotamus spreads its dung on a river-bank the immediate function is to leave a smell that proclaims the hippo's ownership of that area. But there is another, deeper level – namely "What is the survival value of this behavior?" In what way does it help that hippo to breed? Much investigation has taken place in recent years in an attempt to work out how patterns of behavior have evolved, and also how they are good for the individual (adaptive). The branch of ethology known as sociobiology is concerned with looking at the group behavior of animals from this point of view.

ALMOST HUMAN

Some of the work in ethology has given insight into human behavior.

We can see that although we are very complex animals and do things other animals cannot, such as play chess, some aspects of our behavior are directly comparable to those seen in our wild ancestors.

The use of lip and face muscles to express feelings is a good example of this. Care is needed, though, when drawing conclusions about humans from observations on the behavior of other animals. It is an area where many people have made suggestions that may well be interesting but are of no value because they do not have the scientific evidence to back them.

INVESTIGATING BEHAVIOR

To become wholly familiar with an animal's behavior you need to watch it continuously in the wild.

▼ Living in a group is very important to some animals. These baboons enjoy grooming one another. This helps to establish and strengthen friendships between group members.

With several favorable subjects, such as lions on the African plains, it may be possible to keep the animals in view for some time. But in practice, in most types of country, it is almost impossible to watch even a large animal in the wild for very long. Small ones are always likely to disappear into bushes or burrows. Others are active only at night when they cannot be observed without expensive, specialized equipment, such as infrared binoculars.

In some studies it is possible to label the animal you are interested in so that it can be found again. A small radio transmitter may be attached to it or it can be fitted with a collar containing a small amount of radioactive material. Suitable receivers enable the observer to keep track of animals marked in this way. Alternatively an animal's movements may be followed by trapping it at intervals. Markers such as leg rings, fin tags or colored dyes can be used to identify individuals.

When animals are trapped the opportunity is often taken to check their sex and health, and take various measurements such as length and weight. All this information is of interest and may have a bearing on understanding their behavior.

▲ Scientists studying animals in the wild may need to take measurements of them. Here a lion, sent to sleep using a dart gun, is weighed on a small crane.

THE SOCIAL SIDE

Most animals do not act entirely on their own. Many kinds live in groups, whether large or small, and much of their behavior may be concerned with interaction with others in the group. The study of the way in which such social animals react to one another is an enormous subject and much work still needs to be done to find out just how different species arrange their social lives. Even those animals we regard as living alone, like tigers, which spend nearly all the time by themselves, are reacting in some way to their fellow animals, if only by behaving in a way which avoids unwanted meetings.

APPLYING OUR KNOWLEDGE
Helping us to understand our own behavior is just one reason for studying that of wild animals. There are many others: We may be able to discover the best way of deterring pests – how to encourage rats to eat poison bait, for example, or how to drive unwanted birds from airport runways by playing recordings of birds in distress, or by flying hawks to scare them off.

Keeping farm animals so they are healthy, productive and happy is more easily achieved if we understand their behavior. We know that goats will not do well in a field of grass because their behavior and digestive system are tuned to a diet of shrubs and herbs. Knowledge of breeding behavior can also be used to help us. By watching the way they behave, a farmer can tell when a cow or sow is ready to mate and can thus ensure that this happens at the most effective time for fertilization to occur.

ENDLESS FASCINATION
Of the many reasons for studying behavior some have obvious advantages while others are to provide the answers to questions that are less clear. If you asked scientists why they study animal behavior, many would give replies such as "to help us conserve them." But they would also admit that one of their main reasons is simply that behavior is so interesting. Exploring the varied and sometimes curious behavior of the many thousands of species that make up the animal kingdom, is a never-ending source of fascination for scientists just as it can be for anyone who is interested in the natural world.

▲ ▼As well as telling us more about wild animals, behavior studies help us make life better for animals in captivity or on farms. We may prefer to see animals in fields rather than in pens, but if indoor pens are well designed (below) the pigs can carry out all their normal behavior. Here they can root in "earth," scratch against "trees," wallow, and pick dunging sites.

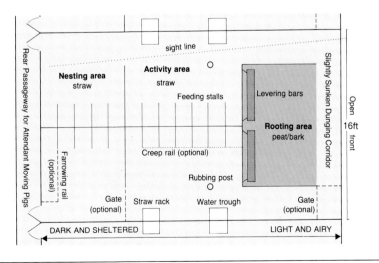

FINDING FOOD

A blowfly lands on a table where there are the remains of a meal. The fly walks across the table and reaches a spot where some sugary fruit juice has been spilt. As its feet contact the sweet liquid it stops and puts down its mouthparts. These consist of a sponge-like tip and a tube up which liquids are sucked. The blowfly has fine hairs on its feet that can "taste" substances. When they find food, then the mouthparts get to work.

Feeding provides many examples of the way in which the shape of animals, their senses and behavior have to fit together to achieve the best result.

THE NEED TO FEED

Every animal has to feed in order to live and grow. None can make its own food. All must get their nourishment either from plants directly, or else at "secondhand" by eating animals that themselves have eaten plants. But food can take a huge number of forms. There are thousands of plants, from almost invisible algae to trees. Possible animal prey can also vary

1

2

5

6

widely in size. Dead plants or animals, or the products of their decay, can also be used as food. Almost every substance that contains organic matter is eaten by some animal somewhere. The range of adaptations for feeding, both in body form and behavior, is enormous. Animals that sustain themselves by killing and eating other animals are dealt with on pages 20 to 25. Those animals that feed on plants or less solid food are dealt with on this and the following pages.

◀▼A variety of feeding techniques
The moose (*Alces alces*) (**1**) browses on vegetation. A goshawk (*Accipiter gentilis*) (**2**) swoops on to its prey. The Common genet (*Genetta genetta*) (**3**) often climbs through trees after its food. The St. Andrew's cross spider (*Argiope aetherea*) (**4**) spins a web to catch prey such as this fly. Greater flamingos (*Phoenicopterus ruber roseus*) (**5**) strain out microscopic organisms from water with their beaks. Butterflies like the Gulf fritillary (*Dione vanillae*) (**6**) suck the nectar from flowers. The squid (*Loligo* species) (**7**) captures fish with the tentacles that encircle its mouth.

3

4

7

THE EASY OPTION

One of the simplest kinds of feeding behavior is shown by those animals called filter feeders. They have some means of sieving tiny plants or animals from the water in which they live. Many groups of animals from sponges to coral, mussels and fanworms use this method. Some fishes, birds and whales are also filter feeders. The behavior of filter feeders can be very simple. They may do little more than stretch out sticky tentacles, as do fanworms, to catch edible objects in the water that flows past. But filter feeding can be more active and complex than this. Mussels, for example, create their own currents of water through their gills to bring more food within reach. From among all of the material suspended in the water they take only some as food and pass it from the gill surface to the mouth. The rest is rejected and passed out of the body in the water current. Particles of the wrong size or taste are discarded.

Many filter feeders, such as fan-worms, do not move about when adult, relying largely on food to come to them. Some bony fish and basking sharks, though, swim through the water with their mouths open. This forces a stream of water through the gills which function as a sieve trap for microscopic food. Blue whales gulp into their mouths a mass of water containing a huge number of small shrimp-like krill, and then use their tongue to push out the water and trap the krill against the frilly plates of horn (baleen) in the roof of the mouth.

MUD PIE
Simply swallowing your surroundings is even less demanding than filter feeding in terms of senses and special behavior, but this indeed is what some earthworms and lugworms do. They swallow mud, and their digestive system acts on any food particles as they go down the gut. The rest is just passed out as waste – worm casts.

GRAZING NOT LAZING
Eating grass would also seem to be a simple option. For an antelope or a buffalo, food is spread out like a carpet under their very noses. At many times of the year it may be plentiful and it would seem that the animal could just walk along like a giant mower eating everything before it. But cattle and other grazers make many choices while feeding. To help them they have their senses of smell and taste, and sensitive lips and whiskers. Some plants are preferred to others. A few, such as buttercups, contain bitter or poisonous chemicals and are avoided. If you look at a pasture where horses have grazed you will see that some plants are well cropped while others are not touched at all.

Even good grass, however, needs to be taken in quite large quantities to provide adequate nourishment. But still it is hard to digest and many grass-eaters rely on bacteria in the gut to ferment it and break it down. Most animals such as cattle "chew the cud" or ruminate, bringing up partly digested food to the mouth for more chewing before sending it back to complete its journey through the gut. Even when ruminants are at rest they are almost constantly chewing, and you can see balls of food traveling up the throat to the mouth at regular intervals. So, even if grazing seems an easy option it involves behavior that may well take up most of the day.

KEEPING MOVING
Many grazing animals keep on the move in the wild so that they do not return to an area too soon before their food has a chance to grow again. In some species, such as wildebeest, long-distance migrations are undertaken to ensure that the herds do not exhaust their feeding grounds. On the other hand, some plants grow back very quickly. Brent geese crop down the marsh vegetation they feed on and then move on. But within 4 days the vegetation has grown back to grazing length again. A Brent goose flock will avoid an area where it has previously fed, but then fly back in about 4 days later to crop it again.

PICK AND MIX
Some plant eaters browse rather than graze. Goats, for example, pick individual leaves, buds or twigs from bushes or tall herbs. Browsers, like grazers, may spend much time in feeding and finding food, though the individual items they eat may be quite nourishing.

▶ In the Red Sea, these corals use the stinging cells on their tentacles to capture small animals to eat. Large fish, such as this grouper, swim over the coral reefs, preying on smaller fish. Microscopic animals, the zooplankton, graze on the tiny plants that drift near the surface of the water.

LIQUID REFRESHMENT

Some of the most specialized plant-eaters are those that feed on nectar from flowers. They include insects such as butterflies, birds, such as hummingbirds, some bats and the Australian Honey possum. Many have long mouthparts or tongues to reach into flowers. They may also use specialized feeding techniques. Hummingbirds hover well, which enables them to feed from otherwise inaccessible flowers. Some animals feed on what may seem to us less appetizing fluids. A few of the most beautiful butterflies, for example, sip pools of liquefying dung on the jungle floor.

FOOD FINDING STRATEGIES

When food is scarce, or occurs only in particular places or at particular times, then behavior that ensures finding it becomes very important. In winter a small bird such as a tit may spend 90 percent of its time searching for food. Many animals, if they encounter one piece of food, will search around thoroughly in the immediate area. For a seed-eating mammal like a wood-mouse this strategy makes sense. Where there is one seed there may well be others.

But knowing when to stop looking is important too. As an animal eats its way through a bush full of berries, for example, the number of food items gradually diminishes and as a result each one will become more and more difficult to find. There must come a point where the animal would be better off looking for another large supply. This point will differ according to whether such supplies are plentiful or not. The behavior of animals seems designed to cope with this. In an area where new supplies are sparse, animals will spend longer using the resource more thoroughly.

Nectar feeders have their feeding strategies too. The amakihi, a bird of the Hawaiian honeycreeper family, remembers where it has fed recently and avoids returning to an area from which it has exhausted the nectar. Bumblebees, when faced with a shortage of flowers, may take the maximum nectar from each. When flowers are plentiful, however, the bees may leave some nectar in every one they visit.

▲ Instead of using its beak to crack seeds, like most other parrots, the Rainbow lorikeet uses the brush-like tip of its tongue to mop up the nectar and pollen from flowers.

1

◄▲Some animals that store food when it is abundant Various species create hoards and return to them when food becomes scarce. Rodents such as the woodmouse (*Apodemus sylvaticus*) **(1)**, store seeds and nuts in part of the burrow when they are plentiful in autumn. Acorn woodpeckers (*Melanerpes formicivorus*) **(2)** drill large numbers of holes in dead trees, then fill them with acorns. The nutcracker (*Nucifraga caryocatactes*) **(3)** stores small collections of food objects in thousands of places within its living area.

Large sized food items, or ones that are most abundant, are not necessarily the best. Small seeds may be easier to open than large ones, or scarce berries may be more nourishing than plentiful ones. Thus, within a given time an animal may get much greater nourishment from small, scarce food items than from larger, more plentiful ones. When we study animal behavior we often find that our subjects are working in the "best" way, not the one that seems to us to be the simplest.

ANIMAL FARM
Humans make reasonably sure of continuing food supplies by growing their own on farms and storing it. Very few animals have developed behavior that could be described as farming, but leafcutter ants do grow their own food, a fungus, in their underground nests. They bring back pieces of leaf into the "gardens" inside the nest and chew them to a pulp on which the fungus grows. Only one fungus type is permitted to grow. If any others appear, the ants weed them out. Some termites are also fungus farmers.

SELECTING A DIET
How do animals select what to eat? For some the body structure and the behavior are so specialized that they are adapted to eating only one kind of food. But many animals have in theory a wide range of possible foods from which to make a choice.

Taste preferences may be important. For people the taste often helps decide whether something is good to eat. This holds for many other animals too. A blowfly prefers some kinds of sugar to others. Some animals are known to acquire a taste for a particular food from their mother. Young rats can recognize something as being good to eat because they have already received traces of its flavor in the mother's milk. Once they start feeding on solids they will show a clear preference for foods the mother had been feeding on.

Other factors can affect preferences too. If a rat falls ill due to the lack of some vital factor in the diet, but is then cured by eating a food that corrects the lack, it may afterwards prefer a diet that contains that food. The same may be true of many other types of animal.

LIVING TOGETHER

A huge fish approaches a coral reef. A small brightly colored fish swims out. The big fish opens its mouth wide. It could easily gulp down the smaller fish but doesn't even try. The smaller fish begins searching the larger one's lips and gills. It even enters the big fish's mouth, stays there a few minutes, and emerges again.

The behavior of fishes at a coral reef "cleaning station" is unusual. Hunting fish come to be cleaned of parasites and do not harm the cleaners. They even spread mouth and gills wide to allow the cleaners to work. Cleaner fish are brightly colored and have a special way of swimming. The behavior of the cleaner and its customer is a good example of symbiosis – a relationship between two species that brings benefits to both. The large fish have their parasites removed, the cleaner fish get a meal.

CROCODILE TOOTHPICK

A similar symbiotic relationship exists between the Nile crocodile and the Egyptian plover. The bird is allowed to scramble over a basking crocodile and even pick scraps of food from its teeth without coming to harm.

A different kind of symbiosis exists between some ants and aphids. The ants "milk" the aphids of their body waste, a sweet liquid called honeydew. They stroke the aphids with their antennae to make them release it. In return for this food the ants may move the aphids to new feeding sites, and will drive off predators. In some species the relationship is so close that an ant queen carries an aphid on her mating flight to ensure continuation of the honeydew supply.

TABLE SCRAPS

There are other types of association between animals. In some cases one benefits from another without doing it either good or harm in return. A gull feeding on a garbage heap, or a raccoon eating from a garbage can, both show behavior that enables them to benefit from associating with people, but without doing harm. This type of relationship is known as commensalism. In some situations, different forms of living together can occur on one animal. For example, as an African buffalo grazes, Cattle egrets hunt for insects it disturbs (commensalism) and oxpeckers search it for tasty parasites (symbiosis).

UNWELCOME GUESTS

Parasitism is, in fact, a third type of relationship. A parasite is an animal that lives in or on another – called the host – at its expense. The parasite survives usually by taking the host's food or by eating or otherwise damaging its tissues, so doing harm. Some

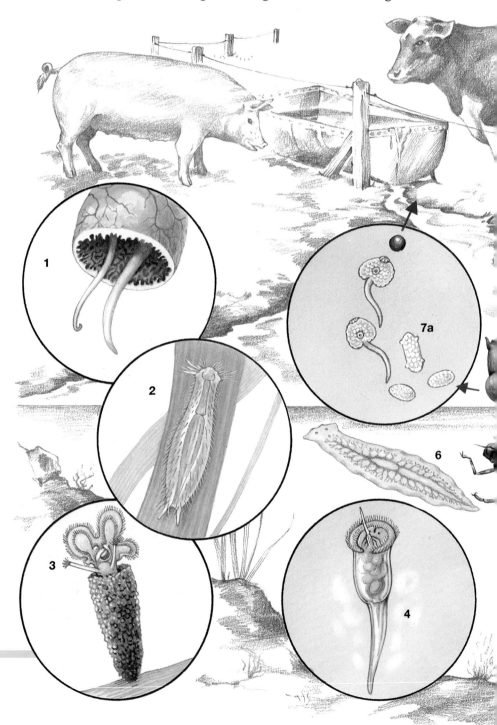

parasites eventually kill their host, but only when they can move on to a free-living stage in their life cycle. Many do not kill the host, however, for they need the host as a permanent home for themselves and perhaps their offspring as well.

A parasite such as a tapeworm living in the gut of a dog or a human needs no special behavior. It fixes itself to its host, and remains in one spot, absorbing nutrients and dissolved

▶A group of ants tends the aphid "cows" that supply them with honeydew. In return the ants provide protection.

▼**Worm-like parasites of farmland and some of their relatives** Living in the gut of the domestic pig is the round worm *Ascaris lumbricoides suilla* (**1**). The gastrotrich *Chaetonotus* (**2**), and the rotifers *Floscularia ringens* (**3**) and *Conochilus hippocrepis* (**4**), prey on bacteria and protozoans, some of which are parasites of mammals. A few rotifers are themselves parasites, as is the worm *Gordius* (**5**), which lives inside aquatic insects. *Dendrocoelum lacteum* (**6**) is a flatworm, some of which depend on symbiotic algae for food. The common liver fluke, *Fasciola hepatica* (**7**), is a parasite of sheep and cattle in Europe. Eggs from the adult fluke develop into larval stages, which first enter a water snail, (**7a**), the secondary host, before reinfecting a primary host. Two more rotifers, a *Branchionus* species (**8**) and *Stephanoceros fimbriatus* (**9**). The flatworm *Dugesia subtentaculata* (**10**).

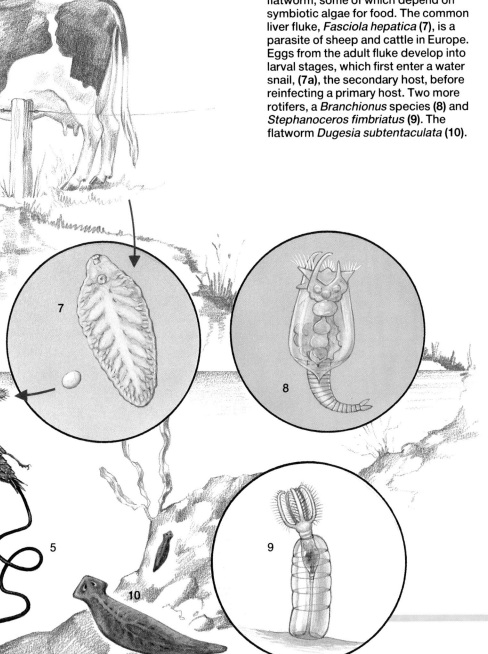

oxygen from the food in which it is bathed. It lacks digestive and blood circulatory systems and sharp senses.

The most important behavior for some parasites is that which gets them or, more importantly, their offspring, to a new host. One flatworm that lives in fishes has to transfer to a bird for one stage in its life cycle. At that time it burrows its way into the fish's eye. This makes the partly blinded fish swim near the surface, thus increasing the chance of being caught by a bird.

TIMING IT RIGHT
The behavior of a parasite is often geared to coincide with that of the host in order to ensure survival. The Rabbit flea, which feeds on its host's blood, breeds in response to the chemicals produced in the blood by a pregnant rabbit. Young fleas therefore emerge just before the young rabbits are born. The increase in body temperature of the mother rabbit at this time makes the fleas more active, and therefore more likely to jump onto the newborn rabbits.

THE HUNTERS

A stalk of dry grass twitches. Over the grass the eyes and ears of a lion gradually appear. It concentrates on the herd of zebra in the clearing ahead. Its tail twitches. Then it suddenly leaps forward and rushes at a zebra. In the whirling dust and confusion the zebra dodges and runs. The lion has missed a possible meal.

Hunting animals, the predators, do not always catch the prey they are after. Lions may succeed in less than a third of their attempts. Leopards may catch their target only once in every twenty hunts. The figures do vary between different species, and at different places, but overall the message is clear – being a hunter is not an easy option.

LOCATING PREY
To find their food, hunters need highly developed sense organs and the ability to use them efficiently. Animals may be able to see, hear or detect faint smells far better than a human. But often a predator will be "tuned in" to particular aspects of the surroundings that betray the presence of prey and may ignore others. Many predators will attack only when they see the prey make a movement.

SIGHT, SMELL OR SOUND?
Some animals react merely to the sight of prey. For example, a praying mantis watches an insect until it is at just the right spot to trigger the mantis to shoot out its front legs and trap it. A chameleon similarly watches with its mobile eyes until the prey is in the right position to be ensnared, this time by shooting out its tongue. Sounds and scents seem to be of little importance to these animals.

For others, however, scent is very important. Wild dogs locate prey in the first place by scent. Snakes follow scent trails by flicking in and out their sensitive forked tongues, "tasting" smells in the air. Some snakes, such as the adder, may pass within sight of their prey but seem to ignore it until the scent trail brings them back to the same spot. It seems that in this situation prey cannot be recognized as such by sight alone.

Other animals use sound as the main information. Some owls are deadly hunters by ear where it is too dark to see. Red foxes and servals may hunt by sound in tall grass, pausing to use their large, spread ears to detect the rustles or squeaks of an otherwise concealed rodent.

"RADAR" SYSTEMS
Sometimes particularly specialized behaviors are used to locate prey. Bats, dolphins and some seals can produce high-pitched sounds and listen for prey by detecting the echoes of these sounds that are bounced back to them. Some fishes generate electric fields in the water. They detect prey by the distortions it produces in these fields. The fishes' behavior maintains their electric field as constant as possible. They keep the body straight and swim only by gently rippling the fins.

HUNTING TECHNIQUES
Once prey is located close at hand, a predator may simply rush it and hope to outrun it quickly. Cheetahs hunt Thomson's gazelles in this way. They must get quite close before the chase can begin, as they can run fast for only 400yd or so. Other cat species need to be even closer. They stalk prey carefully, keeping low and using any plants or rocks as cover, until they are close enough to make a sudden spring or short rush at the prey. Members

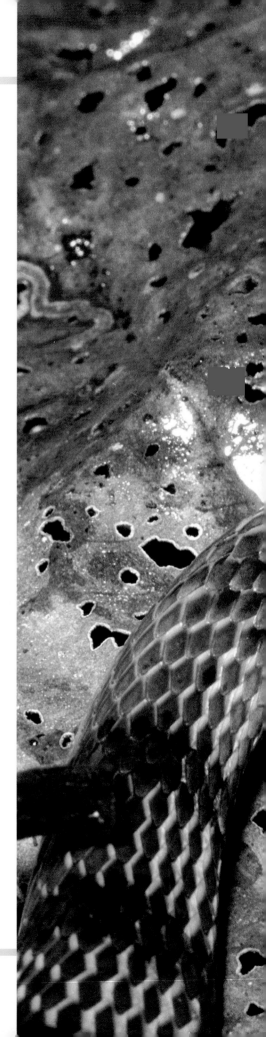

►A Fire-bellied snake eats a harlequin frog. Once they have overpowered prey, snakes maneuver it into the best position for swallowing whole – usually head first.

of the dog family often undertake longer chases, relying on superior endurance rather than speed.

Usually, however, hunters employ energy-saving tactics. A predator will use its past experience to increase its chances of successfully catching prey. It may cut corners in a chase. In many cases very old, sick or young animals are singled out for attack because they are easier to catch and less likely to damage the hunter. Lone animals split off from their herd are also preferred victims because it is difficult for a predator to concentrate on a single animal within a large group.

Even so, chasing or stalking prey can take up much time and energy. Some animals cut down on this by simply waiting in ambush for prey to come by – some snakes do this – or even by building traps. The antlion larva makes a slippery-sided pit in sand and lies in wait buried at the bottom ready to kill insect prey that falls in. Many spiders build webs that snare insects. Some fishes and turtles use their mouths as traps, luring fishes within range by means of a brightly colored tongue or mobile flap of skin on the snout or the chin.

Other animals employ more speculative techniques. Some octopuses, for example, close the web between their tentacles from time to time as they move over rocks and seaweed, and check to see if they have caught anything within.

NOT WHAT THEY SEEM

Some predators deceive prey by mimicking the appearance and initial behavior of harmless species. On the coral reef there are small predatory fish that resemble cleaner fish and imitate their behavior (see page 18). When an unsuspecting fish comes up to be cleaned the predator dashes in and bites off a chunk of flesh.

The Zone-tailed hawk of North America uses a similar deception. It often soars in the company of vultures. Small mammals feel no danger from vultures, and remain unaware of the hawk until it is too late.

DEAD EASY

Not all flesh-eaters hunt living prey. Some, such as vultures, hyenas, jackals, crows and sometimes even lions, avoid the effort by feeding on carrion – animals that have died or been killed by other predators. Seeking them out, by smell or other means, may still be important. Also useful is the ability to interpret the behavior of other animals. If a vulture or jackal sees lions hunting it keeps watch for the kill.

▼ **Methods of detecting prey** Using heat-sensitive pits near the eyes some snakes (1) can detect a temperature rise as small as 0.009°F; this enables them to locate a mouse 6in away in the dark. Bats (2) make high-pitched squeaks and listen to echoes returning from the surroundings, so finding flying insects. Barn owls (3) can hear a mouse moving and catch it in pitch darkness. Hyenas (4) find carrion by smell.

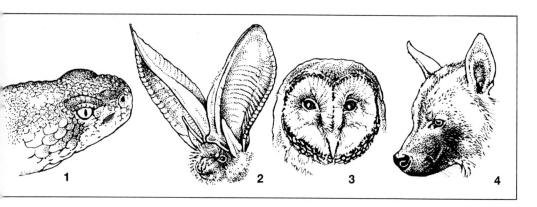

KILLING PREY

Once a predator has captured its prey it needs to subdue it ready for eating. A fox or coyote will pin down a small mammal then aim a killing bite at the head and neck. Violent side-to-side shaking of the head by the attacker helps break the victim's neck and deepen the bite into blood vessels and nerves. Big cats may break a victim's neck with a blow from a paw or may grasp the throat of the prey in their jaws and rapidly suffocate it.

Snakes lack limbs to help overcome prey. Some use their whole body to pin prey down or, as in boas, tightly coil themselves round it to suffocate it. Others have apparently more casual behaviors. Lunging at a cornered victim, they inject it with a powerful venom through specialized teeth and then leave it to wander off and die before following its trail and swallowing the victim. Spiders may wrap prey in silk to stop it moving once it has blundered into a web, after first subduing it with a poisonous bite.

▼Predators and their prey An aardvark (*Orycteropus afer*) (1) licks up termites. A Red-backed shrike (*Lanius collurio*) (2) impales a dead lizard on a thorn. A Gray seal (*Halichoerus grypus*) (3) chases fish. A Herring gull (*Larus argentatus*) (4) chases a Black-headed gull (*Larus ridibundus*) (5) to make it release food which it has taken from a garbage heap. A Noctule bat (*Nyctalus noctula*) (6) homes in on a moth which it has detected by echoes reflected off it.

23

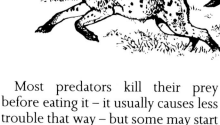

Most predators kill their prey before eating it – it usually causes less trouble that way – but some may start to feed on prey that is still alive. Some insects do this, and a pack of wild dogs will start to tear at a victim before it has stopped struggling.

SUCCESS RATES

Despite all their physical adaptations and their specialized behavior, the predators are by no means always successful in the hunt. Studies have shown that ospreys swooping to the water to catch fish do rather well, with success on 9 out of 10 occasions. A number of predatory fish are equally efficient but for most animals the success rate is much less. At their best, cheetahs and wild dogs may be successful in two out of every three attempts, while kestrels and hyenas may achieve only half this score. Wolves hunting moose were seen to fail 19 times out of 20 – but when they were successful there was plenty for all. All these figures are liable to change at different times and under different conditions. Some individuals are better hunters than others.

Whatever the actual percentage of successful hunts, the behavior of predators usually ensures that enough survive and reproduce. Enough prey survive too for the balance between hunter and hunted to be maintained.

When capturing prey is made artificially easy, a predator's behavior may seem to become extreme. A fox that gets into a chicken roost will kill far more than it is able to eat. Under wild

▼When wolves hunt, one of the pack may work its way round to the front of a herd of caribou while others drive the herd forward to the ambush. The wolves may also try to split one animal from the herd. A sheepdog being worked by a shepherd uses just the same techniques in the service of its master.

▲▶Cooperative killers While one Spotted hyena is chased off by a mother wildebeest, other members of the group chase easier prey – her newly born calf. African hunting dogs chase prey until it is exhausted. Pack members take turns to lead, and through persistence can wear down animals as large as zebra.

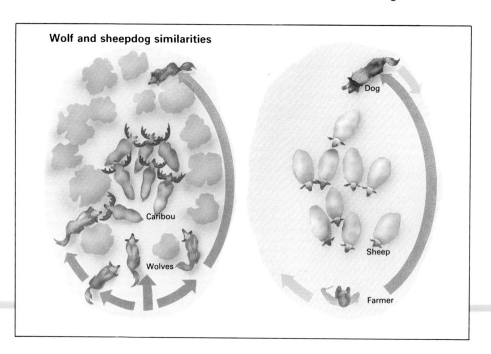

Wolf and sheepdog similarities

Caribou

Wolves

Dog

Sheep

Farmer

conditions such apparently wanton slaughter rarely takes place. Some predators, however, do encounter situations which allow them to catch more meat than they require for their immediate needs. They can then store (cache) the food and return later to continue the feast. A tiger may drag the remains of a carcass into cover and come back for it the next night. If an Arctic fox is able to kill surplus birds it may bury them in the snow. Sometimes they remain in their natural deep-freeze for a long time before the fox needs to dig them out.

FINDING FOOD TOGETHER

Hunting success may increase if the predators get together in groups, even if the individuals are not actively cooperating. A vulture follows others down to the ground because this is a good sign of food being available, but all members of the group have not worked together in getting it.

COOPERATING IN CAPTURE

Some animals, however, show great cooperation when hunting as a group. The members of a pack of wolves work together to achieve a killing. The group spreads out. The individuals chasing the prey in the middle of the group travel more slowly than those on the outside. In this way the prey can be surrounded, making escape difficult. Mammals from wolves to the Killer whale work this way, as do some birds such as pelicans.

Sometimes cleverer tactics are used. Wild dogs and wolves allow one animal to do all the close chasing. It twists and turns after the prey while the rest of the group lopes along on a straighter, shorter path, saving energy. After a spell the lead animal is changed. These tactics can wear down even animals that are faster runners than their hunters. Driving prey towards an ambush is another tactic used by group hunters.

Though some predators hunt in packs others, like the leopard, work alone, relying on cunning. Some species, however, vary their behavior according to the prey. Spotted hyenas may hunt singly, or in twos and threes, for Thomson's gazelles and young wildebeest, but cooperate in a pack of a dozen or more when hunting the much bigger zebra.

Studies show that cooperation greatly increases hunting success. A jackal hunting on its own can catch a Thomson's gazelle – but only once in six attempts. A pair of jackals working together, however, are successful four times out of six.

ANIMAL DEFENCES

A Common toad crossing a meadow is surprised by a snake. The snake moves towards it and the toad responds by puffing itself up with air and straightening its back legs. Suddenly the snake is confronted by an animal that looks at least three times the size of what at first seemed a suitable meal. The snake turns away. The toad has defended itself without a fight.

There are three basic kinds of behavior that an animal can use to defend itself from a predator: it can hide, it can run, or it can fight back. Some animals use a combination of all three methods. Fighting back is probably the least popular option, in terms of actually trading blows or bites, because there is too much risk of getting damaged or even killed. Even animals that do have deadly weapons avoid using them except in desperate situations.

MATCHING THE BACKGROUND

As many predators hunt by sight, an animal that can match its background may avoid detection. A green grasshopper or caterpillar can be very difficult to see on a leaf. But even if an animal is the identical color to its background it may still stand out because its underside, being in shadow, looks darker than the rest. Some animals, such as many deer and fishes, have lighter colored bellies than backs, and this countershading balances the effects of the shadows, making the animal harder to see.

▼The Horned frog, from Malaysia, is camouflaged to resemble a dead leaf on the floor of the rain forest.

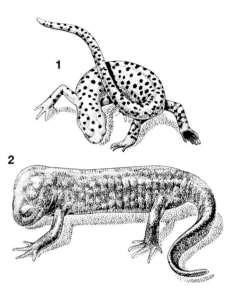

►▼Some defensive postures A Cave salamander (1) holds its body still and waves its long tail. The mole salamander (2) head-butts an enemy and exposes parts of the body with many poisonous skin glands. A Roughskin newt (photo) lifts its head and tail and becomes rigid.

The Frilled lizard makes itself look larger when attacked by spreading wide the collar of skin round its neck.

Other animals reduce shading contrasts by their behavior, flattening themselves down so there is no room for shadows below.

BREAKING OUTLINES

A uniform, blending body color can indeed be good camouflage but even a strikingly patterned body surface is not necessarily conspicuous. If an animal's skin or plumage is made up of differently colored patches it may be very difficult to see as one object. Stripes or patches that cross the outline and break it up are also good camouflage. These patterns tend to work best against a broken up background. A Ringed plover, decked out in its striking pattern of black, white and brown, may be almost impossible to see on a stony beach. But even

▶Threat displays in rodents. The Kenyan crested rat (1) raises its crest, giving off a foul smell from glands beneath it. The Norway lemming (2) lifts its chin to reveal the contrasting pale neck and cheek. The Cape porcupine (3) raises its quills and rattles its tail. If this fails, it stamps its feet or turns and charges in reverse to stab the enemy.

against an almost plain background these patterns can deceive the eye. A herd of zebra on a distant, featureless hillside of short dry grass may not be noticed by a predator.

PLAYING THE PART

There are very many examples of animals that are colored, patterned,

1 2 3 4

▲The Fairy-wren of Australia usually stands upright (1) and moves by hopping along the ground. If it is threatened by an attacker it changes its behavior and runs along the ground with its tail down, squeaking as it goes (2–4). This sudden assumption of a mouse-like appearance can be very effective in distracting a predator and deflecting an attack.

even shaped, in ways that make their camouflage almost perfect. But for it to work they must have the right behavior as well. It is no good matching your background if you go hopping about drawing attention to yourself. Many camouflaged animals become perfectly still when they sense any danger. Even if an enemy approaches they must not panic and move. Some will remain still until the moment they are touched.

Other animals that are camouflaged to resemble their surroundings may display special behavior to enhance the deception. The stick insect may make slow movements and may hold its legs in such a way as to increase its resemblance to a twig. Some twig-like caterpillars hold their body out at just the right angle to match the tiny twigs on their branch. The leaf fish from the mangrove swamps of South America is not only leaf-shaped and covered in brown blotches which mimic those on fallen mangrove leaves, it also rests on its side, just below the surface of the water, in exactly the same way as the real leaves.

SWITCHING DISGUISES
An animal that is camouflaged will become easy to see if the background changes color. Several animals can cope with seasonal changes in their habitat by changing the color of their coats. The stoat, Mountain hare and ptarmigan loose out the brown summer coat and replace it with a white one for the winter so that they remain disguised against the snow-covered ground. In the swallowtail butterfly of North America, the summer caterpillars which live on a rough surface become brown but those on a smooth surface are green, so that the defenseless pupae on different backgrounds will be camouflaged.

QUICK-CHANGE ARTISTS
There are yet other animals that can change color very rapidly. In these the color pigment in the skin cells is under the control of nerves or chemicals in the body. The animal's behavior and the location it is in influence the color. Some crabs can vary their color over a few days to fit in with new surroundings. Some lizards such as anoles and chameleons are famous for their color changes, which may take only a few minutes or seconds as pigments of various colors spread or contract within their skins. These animals may change color with changing moods, but are also good at matching the colors and patterns of natural backgrounds.

Another group of animals with color-changing ability are the flatfishes. Plaice and flounders can change within seconds of moving from a light to dark background on the sea bottom. Some match not only the color but also the pattern and apparent texture of the sand or gravel on which they rest.

RUN FOR YOUR LIFE
What happens if you are camouflaged, but a hunter finds you anyway, or comes so close he must stumble over you? A few animals try to stick it out. An opossum may "play dead" even if nudged. Many predators attack only moving prey, so it may escape. But for most animals the response to discovery is immediate flight, getting away as far and as fast as possible. For many animals running away is the normal response to danger. Sometimes there is a definite distance, the "flight distance," which they try to maintain between themselves and danger. An enemy is tolerated if further away, but once within the flight distance it will trigger escape reactions. Flight distances can vary depending on the hunting techniques of the predator. Thomson's gazelles, for example, may run away from African hunting dogs at a range of 1,000yd, but sometimes will allow a cheetah to come as close as 100yd before they begin to show concern.

Gazelles, antelope and zebra run from trouble, but several smaller animals can seek refuge in burrows and other places. A frightened rabbit dives for its burrow. A squirrel will scamper up a tree away from a hunter on the ground. A fanworm withdraws into its tube. A clam shuts its two shells tight. Even animals such as this may respond differently to different predators. Most threats simply make a scallop close up, but if it senses the presence of starfish (which can pull shells apart) it will swim off by clapping its shells together in a kind of jet propulsion.

Caterpillar defenses
◄The distasteful Death's head hawkmoth caterpillar has distinctive markings. Any predator that attacks one once is unlikely to repeat the attack on similarly marked creatures in future. The species as a whole gains protection, even though some individuals must die.

▼Some caterpillars, like this one, gain protection from predators by resembling a bird dropping.

FLASH COLORS

If an animal cannot get away from a predator it may try to confuse its pursuer in order to make capture more difficult. Many moths, such as the Yellow underwing, have bright colors on the hindwing. At rest these colors are hidden, but if the moth is disturbed it flies away quickly, exposing the bright yellow flashes on its hindwings as it goes. When it lands the yellow disappears as the wings close, and a predator is left confused. Many insects, including some grasshoppers, have the same kind of defense mechanism. Among the tree frogs are a number of species that are generally well camouflaged, but have vivid colors on the inside of the legs. When they are sitting on a branch or leaf these cannot be seen, but if they are attacked and jump away, a flash of color attracts attention, then disappears as they land.

Being colored and shaped so as to distract a predator's attention away from important organs is another safeguard. The Peacock butterfly has large eye markings on the wing tips.

Eye shapes attract attention and a bird in search of a meal may aim its snap at the most obvious bit of the butterfly – an "eye" – and miss the head and body. The strategy works, for Peacock butterflies are sometimes seen flying around with body intact but with notches pecked out of the wing. Other butterflies, including many of the browns, and some moths also have eye markings. In some tropical blue butterflies there are both false eyes and false antennae which direct attention to the wrong end of the animal. When it flies off it moves in the opposite direction to that expected by the attacker. Many fishes have "eyes" at the wrong end too.

THE LAST STAND

If all else fails, the final defense of most animals is to stand and fight with whatever weapons are available. Horns, teeth and claws may all be used. Some animals have stings or poisonous bites. Others are distasteful or have poison glands in the skin. But in most cases, if an enemy comes close enough for these weapons

to be brought into play, there is a danger that their owner may be hurt before or while using them. Even if you have a powerful weapon, it is far better to advertise the fact and try to scare off an enemy first. A porcupine puts on a warning display instead of stabbing at an attacker with its quills immediately. A skunk has a very powerful weapon, a nauseatingly smelly fluid it can spray from scent glands under the tail. It rarely has to use it, however, because its black and white color, its lack of fear, and its threats, are usually enough to scare off most trouble.

COLOR CODING

Foul-tasting animals are often brightly colored. The black and yellow bands of the Cinnabar moth caterpillar, and the black and red of the adult are signals that they are not tasty. The Common salamander of Europe, which has poison glands in the skin, is also yellow and black, and many other amphibians, such as poison-arrow frogs, have bright colors to advertise the fact they are distasteful.

Once a predator has tried attacking or eating something with warning coloration it is unlikely to do so again. A few individuals do become victims, but the strategy is effective for the species as a whole. Animals with warning colors, as you may expect, are often far less "shy" than those which lack this form of protection.

Some species of predator seem to avoid warning colors automatically. Great kiskadees and motmots, birds from North America, will avoid even sticks painted with red, black and yellow bands. Most birds, though, seem to learn about warning colors through their own experiences.

UNDER FALSE PRETENSES

Warning colors are possibly most useful to fairly common species. In a rare species, too high a proportion of individuals would be killed by inquisitive predators. But if many species share the same warning color, fewer of each will be killed before the message gets through to the predators. All over the world there are various kinds of wasps patterned in the same black and yellow to advertise their stinging ability.

Some harmless species gain a defense by imitating the dangerous ones in appearance and behavior. Hoverflies have no sting, but are patterned like wasps and bees. They behave similarly too, buzzing about and visiting flowers like bees. They are good enough imitations to fool many people, as well as would-be predators. In the Americas several species of harmless snake mimic the highly venomous coral snakes. There are mimics among the butterflies too, with many pairs of species where one is distasteful and another imitates it in appearance and the way it flies.

▼The colorful pattern of the harmless King snake (large photo) may protect it. It mimics that of the venomous Coral snake (inset). Predators avoid colors that they associate with danger.

MIGRATION

Somewhere in southern Britain a radar operator watches the screen in front of him. As the radar sweeps a circle in the sky the man can see blips of light showing thousands of invaders coming from the skies of continental Europe. But he knows they are completely harmless. They are radar images of starlings migrating west in the fall.

Most animals move about during their lifetime. Some spend their whole lives within a small area. A shrew may be constantly on the move, but never leaves an area larger than a few tens of square yards. Other animals travel hundreds or even many thousands of miles during their lifetime in movements we call migrations.

WHAT IS MIGRATION?

Several different kinds of animal journey are sometimes called migration. Some of these journeys are one-way movements. Many scientists prefer to use the term migration only for long-distance seasonal movements to different feeding grounds, or between breeding and wintering areas.

ONE-WAY TICKETS

Overpopulation, causing lack of food or breeding space, is one of the reasons for mass movements. Locusts may be relatively harmless animals, but the build-up of young ones in an area can sometimes act as a trigger that starts the swarming behavior. Then huge masses of adult locusts take to the wing, moving across a whole continent and destroying crops as they go. Lemmings often march in

▶ Even a large river is not enough to deter a herd of wildebeest on migration. Each year, herds many thousands strong move regularly with the seasons to take advantage of the growth of grasses in the different parts of their range.

hordes in those years when they have a sudden population explosion.

Some birds from Northern Asia, such as waxwings, crossbills and Siberian jays, also have exceptional years in which the enlarged population spreads from its normal area. Birds from Siberia may even end up in Western Europe. Some may return, but others colonize new areas or die out. Such movements are usually known as "irruptions," and this is probably a better term than migration for these one-way movements.

ROUND TRIPS
In East Africa millions of wildebeest make a huge circular trip each year round the grasslands of the Serengeti plains. Although close to the equator, the area experiences seasonal changes in rainfall which result in a flush of new grass at different times in different areas. The wildebeest keep on the move to make the best use of the new grass as it appears.

In Canada, great herds of caribou move up into the Arctic tundra in the summer, then travel back more than 500mi to the south as winter starts. Once again, they are making use of the seasonal wealth of food.

On a smaller scale, many amphibians such as newts and frogs migrate. They move from winter quarters on the land to their breeding ponds.

▼Some Humpback whales (like those photographed here off the Alaskan shore) spend the summer months feeding in the far north of the Pacific and Atlantic Oceans. In the northern winter they migrate to equatorial regions where they breed. Others occupy the Southern hemisphere and undertake a similar migration (map). Because the hemispheres have opposite seasons, the two populations never mix.

Summer feeding grounds   Winter breeding grounds

→ Migration routes

Though of short duration the migrations may be spectacular because of the sheer numbers involved. A few species travel several miles, a surprising distance for such small, slow-moving creatures. In some places in Britain tunnels have been built as "underpasses" for toads, to help them cross busy roads safely.

The spectacular migrations that salmon undertake are also linked to their reproduction. The eggs must be laid in the well-oxygenated, clean water of the upper parts of rivers. As the salmon grow, however, they migrate downstream. They move far out to sea where they feed for up to 10 years. When they are ready to breed large mature adults find their way back, nearly always to their birthplace, continuing up-river past waterfalls and other difficult obstacles.

FOLLOWING FOOD

How far a species migrates often depends on the availability of its food. A seed-eating bird may need to migrate only a short way to find conditions where it can survive the winter. An insect eater, though, needs to be in a climate where it can rely on its food. So a swallow or swift may migrate from northern Europe all the way to southern Africa in the winter when insects in its breeding area are scarce. Hummingbirds can live in the northern USA in summer but falling temperature and lack of flowers with nectar force them to fly many miles south for winter.

Many long-distance migrants take advantage of the local summers of each hemisphere in turn. The Arctic tern lives and breeds within the Arctic circle in the northern summer, then goes south as far as the Antarctic coasts for the southern summer. This regime allows it to enjoy long days and an abundant food supply throughout most of the year.

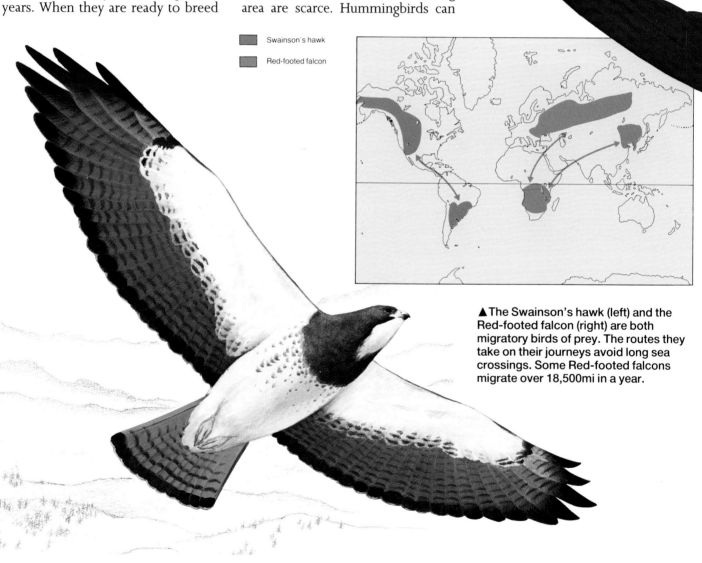

Swainson's hawk

Red-footed falcon

▲The Swainson's hawk (left) and the Red-footed falcon (right) are both migratory birds of prey. The routes they take on their journeys avoid long sea crossings. Some Red-footed falcons migrate over 18,500mi in a year.

MYSTERY MIGRATIONS

European eels start life in the Sargasso Sea in the western Atlantic. The larvae develop as they move across the Atlantic and after 3 years they all reach European rivers. They swim up the rivers and spend several years feeding and growing. Then they reach breeding condition and begin the migration back. But it has never been proved that these adults complete the crossing, against the North Atlantic Drift, back to the breeding grounds. Some people believe that all the breeding adults in the Sargasso Sea come from the American continent.

Another mystery migration is that of the Green turtles of Ascension Island in the middle of the South Atlantic. The turtles breed on the island but they feed off the coast of Brazil. How they travel between these two areas is completely unknown. In one direction they would be swimming against ocean currents which exceed the turtle's swimming speed. Perhaps they take a roundabout route, but nobody knows.

▲North American Monarch butterflies fly thousands of miles south and overwinter in masses in valleys in Mexico, Florida and California.

▼These transparent eel larvae ready to swim up a European river, took several years to cross the Atlantic since hatching in the Sargasso Sea (map).

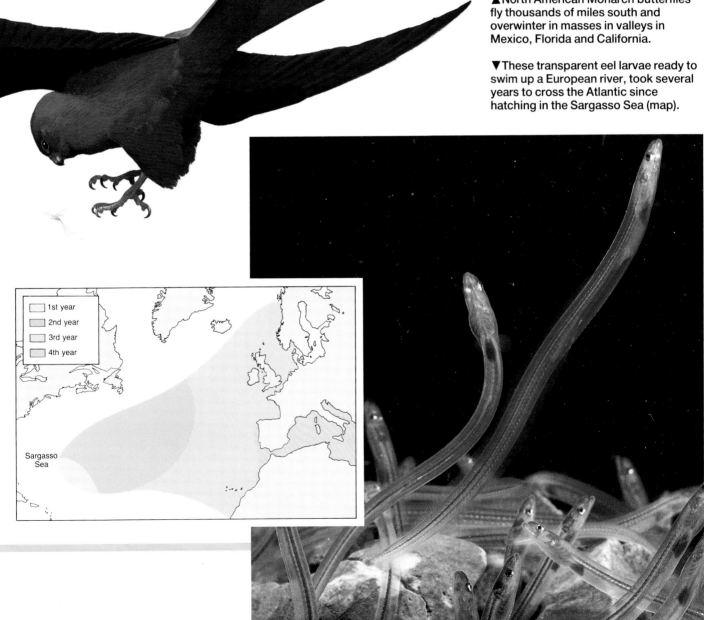

1st year
2nd year
3rd year
4th year

Sargasso Sea

NAVIGATION

A lorry draws up. The back is full of baskets of pigeons. The driver releases the birds. They take off and climb fast. They circle briefly, then, with scarcely a pause, set off purposefully in the direction of home. Before the lorry has time to complete the return journey all the racing pigeons have covered the 130mi to their home lofts.

Homing pigeons provide one of the most spectacular examples of navigational ability among animals, but they are not unique. Most animals, even some of the simplest, possess some ability to find "home" or steer about their familiar surroundings.

KEEPING IT DARK

Some animals can find their way by responding very simply to changes in their surroundings. Woodlice instinctively move away from light. By doing this they end up in crevices or under stones which form a moist, protective home. Worms too may move away from light, a reaction that sends them back in the right direction if they become exposed on the surface of the ground. Even some complex animals find this sort of simple response useful in their orientation. Turtles hatch at night and find the safety of the sea by heading off towards the brighter part of their surroundings (see page 39).

In some cases much more complicated reactions guide animals in their movements or their return to a base. A limpet returns to its own particular home spot on a rock after a feeding expedition. A badger returns to its sett after a night of foraging that may cover hundreds of yards. A whole combination of factors helps such animals to reach home. The familiar smell of home may play a part, and animals such as badgers leave their

▲ Planetaria can be used to expose birds to the night-time sky patterns seen at different places or times of year. This may show when the migratory instinct is strongest or whether birds could compensate if blown off course.

scent marks at intervals so they can find their way back along their own trail. Wild animals, like people, may also develop a mental "map" of their surroundings. This gives them a good idea where they are at any one time.

Many animals also seem to have the ability to memorize, unconsciously, the movements they have made during an expedition, so they can retrace their footsteps to get back to a place they recognize. Some people too have this same ability to navigate by recognizing the direction and the distance traveled, while in others this sense is poorly developed.

LANDMARKS

Sometimes other animals seem to navigate in the most common way that we use – by sight. We recognize particular features of the surroundings and take our directions from them. Birds use the same ability when in a familiar area. Many insects, including bees and digger wasps (see page 38), may also use visual landmarks to recognize their own nest entrances. Patterns in the terrain help animals such as elephants and antelopes on the plains of Africa to find their way about, even though their surroundings may seem featureless to us.

EXPERIENCE TELLS

Experience is a major factor in becoming skilled at finding your way about. An area will never become familiar until you have explored it. A young honeybee taken a short distance from its hive becomes lost but an older, more experienced bee can get back from several miles away.

▲ ▼ Racing pigeons can find their way home over long distances. There is evidence that they can navigate using a combination of any of the following methods: the Sun (1); remembering the route on the outward journey (2); smells (3); the Earth's magnetic field (4); and familiar landmarks near home (5). Which sense is most important at any one time seems to differ according to the conditions, but for successful navigation more than one is used.

Experiments have revealed that migratory birds can also improve their navigational performance with experience. Birds flying just south of west through Holland on their fall migration from eastern Europe were caught. They were taken south to Switzerland and released. The young birds in the group, who were on their first migration, carried on in the original direction and ended up in Spain. The older birds readjusted their direction of flight and successfully arrived at their normal wintering areas in France and England.

BUILT-IN MAPS

Experiments such as this show that a young migratory bird carries some sort of built-in information that enables it to make its first long migration. This has to be so, because in many bird species such as swallows the adults start their migration earlier than do their young. With no parental example to guide them, how do the juveniles know where to go?

If we accept that the young birds somehow possess information on the distance and direction of their destination, even though they have never been there before, how do they put it into effect on the journey? In their first weeks of life, before the compulsion to migrate arises, they pick up information that orientates them in their daily lives. They acquire the ability to "know" which is north and which is south. An appreciation of direction similar to our own understanding of the points of the compass is clearly important because the actual line of the migration is not necessarily straight. For example, for a young Garden warbler, hatched in central Europe and migrating via Spain to central Africa, the necessary flight plan might be "fly 6 weeks south-west, then 8 weeks south-south-east".

GETTING YOUR BEARINGS

Experiments with young birds raised without seeing the sky have shown that some at least can use the Earth's magnetic field as a reference system for directions. But many night-time migrants can use information from star positions as well. Just as we can find north by the Pole star and its nearby constellations, so birds seem able to travel in the right direction by reference to the starlit night sky. Birds may be able to use both these types of clue either independently or together.

Some migrants use the Sun to help them orientate, but experiments suggest that for many daytime migrants it is not important. The setting Sun may help to label the west for some night migrants, however.

SUPERSENSES

Some of the navigational ability shown by other animals may depend on senses which we do not possess. The ability to detect magnetic fields, for example – something that we cannot do – has been shown in a range of animals from pigeons to bees. If an animal can detect the Earth's magnetic field it can tell north from south. Also, if it is very sensitive, it may be able to detect the direction of the field in relation to the ground (the "dip") and thereby tell how far north or south of the equator it is at the time. Most animals investigated so far, however, cannot do more than use magnetism as a simple compass.

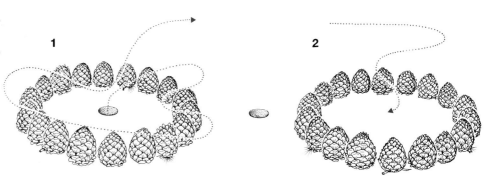

▲ How a wasp recognizes its front door. A ring of pine cones was placed round the hole of a digger wasp. When it left the nest (1) it flew round memorizing key features. Before the wasp came back, the cones were moved (2). It landed in the circle of cones, not beside the nest hole.

▼ Elephants build up a "map" in their memory that helps them find their way around, even in countryside that to us seems to have few distinctive features.

Another cue that may be used by other animals, but which we cannot detect, is very low-frequency sound. It is believed that some species may be able to detect the whereabouts of particular features such as mountains by the sounds made by wind blowing over them. Noises like these may be detectable from many thousands of miles away.

Other species use visual cues that we cannot see. Many insects can see ultraviolet light, or are sensitive to polarized light. Bees use the position of the Sun as a reference point when finding their way about. Because their eyes are tuned in a different way to ours, they can "see" where it is in the sky even when it is clouded over.

We know that some animals find their way by smell, and in some this sense is millions of times more sensitive than our own. Salmon find their way back from the ocean to the river where they hatched by detecting the characteristic smell of the water at the river mouth. As they go upriver they can even choose the right feeder stream by its smell.

FAILSAFE SYSTEMS

Some animals often use more than one system to find their way. Many experiments have been done with pigeons because their homing skills are so good and they are easy to work with. Much of their ability is still not properly understood, but they seem to be capable of navigating in several ways. They have a good memory for local features and can also make use of smell, one sense that is generally not well-developed in birds. They sometimes remember the twists and turns of an outward route as well. For long-distance navigation they rely heavily on the Sun and the Earth's magnetic field.

If pigeons are released on a sunny day they soon turn and make for home. If the day is overcast they do the same. But if they are released on an overcast day, and with little magnets attached to them to upset their senses, they are unable to orientate correctly and set off in random directions.

It seems that they can use either the Sun or the magnetic field to work out their orientation, but if they are denied the information from both these sources they are unable to determine which way to go. They fly aimlessly around the release point and usually remain in the area until either the Sun reappears or they are captured and the magnets removed.

LONG-DISTANCE NAVIGATION

Experiments with marked birds have produced some remarkable navigational feats. A Leach's petrel, taken from the coast of Maine in the east of the USA to England, found its way back home. The shortest distance it could have flown was 3,000mi, but it made the flight in 2 weeks. Even more impressive were the journeys of the Laysan albatrosses that were taken from Midway Island in the middle of the Pacific Ocean and released 4,000mi away. They found their way back to this one tiny dot in the vastness of the Pacific. The birds were artificially moved in these experiments but, of course, comparable feats of navigation are performed by many migratory birds every year.

▲ ▼ ▶ When Green turtles hatch on the sandy beaches of Ascension Island, their first challenge is to find their way down to the sea. As they struggle across the moonlit sand many fall prey to predators. They know instinctively which way to head, reacting to the brightness over the sea, which reflects more light than the land behind them. Having paddled wildly to reach the sea they swim out to the relative safety of deep water. Migrating adults (map right) may navigate by taking their bearings from the Sun.

It is early morning in a Central American forest. From the distance comes a sound like rumbling thunder. But this sound is produced by a small troop of Howler monkeys high in the trees. They are signaling their presence to others in the forest. Soon the members of a troop a mile away cry back in answer.

For many wild animals, as for humans, sound is a very important means of communication. But there are other forms of "language" too. Some of our own communication is by sight. We take note of the expressions on people's faces, their gestures and the way they stand. Even though our noses are not highly efficient there is evidence that we also respond to scents produced by other people.

Other animals, too, can react to all these types of communication. Some may be able to communicate by yet other means. Some fishes, for example, respond to electrical signals. The signals that are important vary among species, according to their senses and the places they live.

SIGNALS BETWEEN SPECIES

We think of communication as taking place mainly between individuals of the same species, but sometimes different species need to "talk" to each other as well. The warning coloration of venomous animals is an example of one species getting a message across to another. You do not have to be another dog to know that a growling, snarling dog is best avoided. Warning growls and the baring of teeth are common expressions of aggressive behavior among mammals, and are understood across the species divide.

Warning displays are used as "keep off" notices by some nesting birds. These can communicate a deceptive message. The Cut-throat finch of

Africa is small and harmless, but if disturbed on its nest it will open its mouth and writhe its neck about in an intimidating, snake-like display which is usually enough to put off any curious intruder.

GENERAL ALARM

Alarm calls are another type of signal that often works across the species barrier. Many birds have rather similar alarm calls – thin, high-pitched and difficult to locate. Other kinds of bird may react to them. Among species that associate together, the alarm call of one may alert the others. Indeed, for some this may be the main advantage of the association.

SIGNALING YOUR SPECIES

The sole function of some animal communication is to allow different

▶ Gannets live in packed colonies and need clear signals to communicate and maintain order. In the background, behind bickering neighbors, two pairs stretch their necks in greeting.

▲ A klipspringer marks the boundary of his territory with secretions from a gland in front of the eye. The black blob of secretion shows this twig has been used many times before.

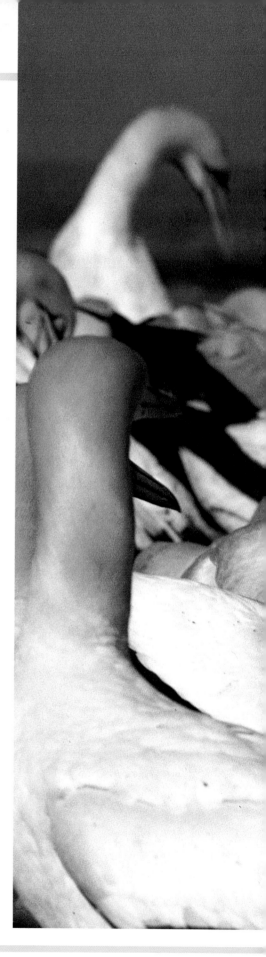

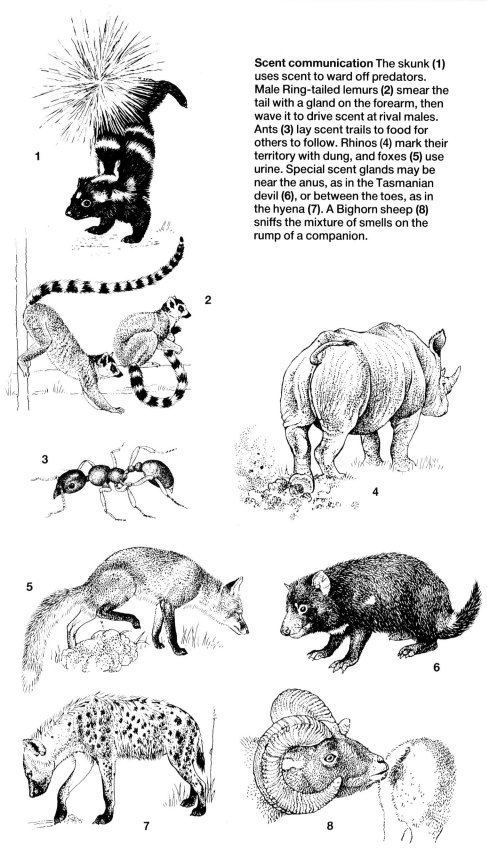

Scent communication The skunk (1) uses scent to ward off predators. Male Ring-tailed lemurs (2) smear the tail with a gland on the forearm, then wave it to drive scent at rival males. Ants (3) lay scent trails to food for others to follow. Rhinos (4) mark their territory with dung, and foxes (5) use urine. Special scent glands may be near the anus, as in the Tasmanian devil (6), or between the toes, as in the hyena (7). A Bighorn sheep (8) sniffs the mixture of smells on the rump of a companion.

individuals to recognize one another as the same species. Many birds can tell their own kind by the color and pattern of their feathers. Different fish species of similar shape and size may have easily recognized colors.

Sometimes the recognition signals are confined to small areas of the body. A penguin swims low in the water, so most of its body cannot be seen by others swimming with it. Its species "badge" is therefore restricted to the only really visible parts – the head and neck. An orange collar, a yellow crest, different face markings – all are used as distinguishing features between the various species.

Most of the species of guenon monkey in Africa are rather similar, but each one has a characteristically different face, either in color or in adornment with special features such as moustaches or nose spots.

"TALKING" TOGETHER

Most other animals communicate general messages rather than precise words and sentences as we do. They may signal their mood, their sex, their readiness to mate, and so on. Many of the signals are very stereotyped and cannot contain shades of meaning. A male stickleback in mating condition keeps his red belly through the breeding season, sending out a constant generalized message that proclaims simply his sex and maturity.

There are many species in which the sexes are different colors. This is a common phenomenon in birds, where the female is often camouflaged for protection, but males may be quite gaudy, as in the Common pheasant. Even where sexes are patterned alike, the male bird will often be brighter than the female.

Among the mammals it is more unusual for the sexes to be differently colored. Some monkeys, however, do use this form of communication – the male mandrill, with his bright blue and red nose, is a good example.

▲ Many whales communicate by sound. It travels well through the water, and keeps whales in touch over thousands of miles. Humpback whales have a long complex "song," made up of chirps, groans, snores, ees and yups.

▼ The Plainfin midshipman is a fish from the Pacific Ocean. By day it burrows in mud on the bottom. Its repertoire of signals includes grunts, growls and whistles, as well as the luminous spots which form a pattern in its skin.

MULTIPURPOSE SIGNALS

The same signal can mean different things to different listeners. Although it may be identical every time, the song of a male bird can be interpreted in a number of ways depending on who hears it. It tells the species of bird. It signals that the bird is male. It may have a personal touch that identifies the bird as a particular individual. A neighboring male reads the signal as "please keep away" but a female may read it as an invitation to mate.

GROUP COMMUNICATION

Animals that live in social groups need signals that help to keep the group together, or to coordinate their movements. Many deer have light-colored rump patches – an easy feature for other group members to follow. Many antelope have pale rumps or tails that are picked out in white and black. Again, these are easy to see at comparatively short range, and an antelope with its face to the ground feeding is still able to keep track of other members of its group out of the corner of its eye. Many birds have white bars on the wings or tail which are easy for their fellows to notice and recognize, even at a distance.

Sounds can also be used to maintain contact. Feeding parties of birds twitter to keep in touch as they forage through the trees. The "stomach rumble" of elephants is also thought to be a contact call between members of a group, signaling the individual's presence and well-being. A herd of wildebeest contentedly grazing keeps up a continual mutter of the sound "gnu, gnu" that has given them their alternative name.

CRESTS AND SPOTS

Some markings emphasize the parts of the body that an animal uses for signaling. Lions show their mood by the disposition of ears and tail. When annoyed, a lion puts its ears back and swishes its tail. Unlike the rest of the

body, which is camouflaged brown, the back of the ears and the tip of the tail have black fur to reinforce the visibility of the signals. Other members of the cat family have ear spots or tufts for the same reason.

Cockatoos use head movements as signals. These are emphasized by crests that can be raised when the birds are excited. Cranes dance to one another, bowing their heads and holding out the wings. These parts of the body are often specially colored for emphasis. The Crowned crane has white underwings, and a colored and crested head that contrast with the gray body. The eyelids and brows of some monkeys are colored to emphasize facial expressions.

IMPORTANT INFORMATION

As well as communicating to describe mood or status, some animals can also relate specific information about the world around them to others of their kind. The alarm calls of birds say "predator about" to other birds. Some kinds of fishes produce an alarm substance – a chemical that they release into the water when they are hurt or badly frightened – that alerts other fish in the school to possible danger. Mammals too may produce scents when they are frightened.

There are also calls that mean "food is here." For many animals this information is best kept to themselves, but for those that live in groups there may be advantage in directing all group members to a supply.

WAYS OF SENDING MESSAGES

Most animals communicate by sight, sound or smell. Each way has its own merits. Sound radiates in all directions and it can be heard a long way off. It performs even better in water. The song of a Humpback whale can be heard at least 750mi away. Its properties make sound a good signal for "advertising" for a mate. The croaking of frogs, the chirping of grasshoppers, and the song of birds are examples. Alarm messages also can be given efficiently using sound, such as the thump of a rabbit's foot, or the alarm bark of a deer.

Visual signals travel even faster than sounds, but obstacles can get in the way. Sight may not be effective for long-distance communication but is good for "private" communication at short range, as in courtship displays.

The last of the three main senses, smell, might seem to us a poor means of communication. But, by producing some special chemicals known as pheromones, animals can give quite complicated messages in smells. In mongooses, and probably many other mammals too, each individual has its own scent by which others can recognize it. Some individual fish signal how aggressive they are by their scent. Moths use pheromones to advertise for mates. A tiny amount of scent is released by a female in mating condition. Males of the same species are sensitive to as little as a few molecules of the chemical and can follow the wind-borne trail over long distances

▲ The communication signal of the male Great frigatebird is a startling red pouch which can be blown out with air.

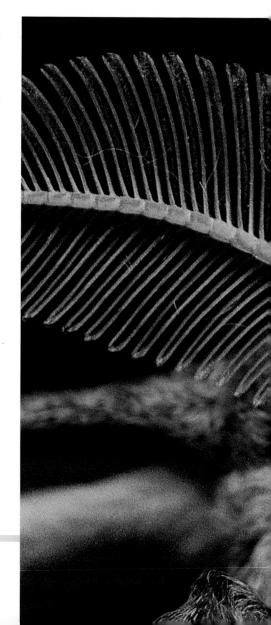

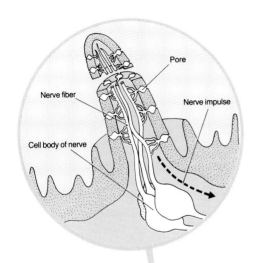

Nerve fiber

Pore

Nerve impulse

Cell body of nerve

back to its source. This means of communication has a far greater range than any sound or visual signal that such a small animal might be able to produce or display.

LIMITED LANGUAGE

Although other animals use many different signaling systems none can communicate the kind of complex information which is encoded in

▼ The use of scent is very important for communication in some moths. The female African silkworm moth produces scent which the male can detect from several miles away. The feathery antennae detect the scent. The inset photos and diagram show the sensory hairs on the antennae greatly magnified.

human language. Those animals that come closest, as might be expected, are the ones which have a complex social organization. Monkeys and apes have an extensive repertoire of facial expressions, grunts and calls, but nothing like speech. However, they may be able to communicate more detailed information to one another than most animals can. Bird alarm calls contain just a general warning, but the Vervet monkey gives a different call for a leopard, an eagle or a snake, and the other Vervets in the group take appropriate evasive action. Some social insects, such as bees, are also able to pass on precise information to their fellows by means of elaborate body movements.

TERRITORY

A male fish swims above a nest hollow in the lake floor. Another male approaches and suddenly there is a flash of fins as the first one chases the intruder. But then the second fish turns on its pursuer, for it is now close to its own nest. Then the two fish face one another, motionless, across an invisible barrier. Each is at the limit of its territory.

▼Female kob antelope move across a river floodplain. In the breeding season the horned males establish mating territories (called "leks," see inset map) in the areas most used by females. They compete for the females' attention.

A territory is an area defended against intruders of the same species by an individual or a group. Animals may defend their territories by fighting or by chasing intruders away. Often, though, a simple signal that they are in occupation is enough to make other members of the species avoid the area. Signals for this purpose may include visual displays, but scents or sounds, such as the songs of birds or the cries of howler monkeys, are often more important.

WHY HAVE A TERRITORY?
Owning a territory gives an animal the exclusive use of some important resource within it. This may be a food supply, it may be a partner with which

High ground

A single lek

0   220yd

to mate, or it may be a suitable site for a nest or a burrow. In many birds, such as the Blue tit and the European robin, the male takes up his possession of a territory by early spring. He entices a mate into it, and the area he defends provides sufficient space for nesting and for finding the food needed to bring up a family.

Groups of Vervet monkeys on the African savannah are territorial. For them, one of the most important features that a territory must have is a reliable waterhole.

Some animals, such as the hartebeest and kob antelope, use territory just for the purpose of mating. During the breeding season males defend pieces of ground that are too small to

▲A confrontation in a tropical forest
Two groups of African Redtail monkeys (*Cercopithecus ascanius*) meet at the edge of their adjoining territories. The adult females and juveniles (1) cluster together to face and threaten members of a neighboring troop (2). During the tension, group members often take time out to groom one another (3), perhaps helping individuals to feel closer and more secure. Although threat gestures are intense and the monkeys make a lot of noise, physical contact between the groups is rare. An adult male (4) may stay well away from the squabble.

47

▲A group of male cheetahs attack a wandering male that has trespassed into their territory on the Serengeti plains in Tanzania. Outsiders intruding in this way can expect to be attacked and driven away or even killed.

◄The Painted snipe is an unusual bird in that the female mates with several males. She establishes a territory and makes hooting calls to attract males. Rival females are frightened away by this extended wing display.

►Cape gannets live in colonies of up to 100,000 individuals, but each pair holds a small territory around its nest. Here the pair on the right defend their nest against an intruder. Pairs are so densely packed that there is a constant hubbub of such squabbles.

feed even a single adult, but they get exclusive mating rights to any female entering them. Other animals have movable territories. Impala antelope males change their territories as the herds change their grazing grounds, and so do other migratory species such as wildebeest.

VARIABLE SIZES

The size of a territory depends on what it is needed for and where it is. A kob holds a small area. Other species that use territory just for mating also defend relatively small areas. That of the male Sage grouse of America, for example, is a circle only 15 to 35ft in diameter on a display ground used by several birds.

A territory that contains all the food necessary for a pair to rear young may be large, particularly if the food is difficult to find. So a pair of eagles or a pack of wolves range over an area of several square miles that they try to keep for their exclusive use. Even a small bird like a nuthatch requires a feeding territory up to 650ft across. In poor habitats territories need to be bigger than in rich ones. The dunlin, a small wading bird, can manage in southern Alaska with a territory as small as 350 sq yd, whereas high in the Arctic it may need one five times this area if it is to survive.

Thus territory sizes vary from a single puddle, in the case of some male frogs, to over 40 sq mi in the case of some of the big cats. Even within a species there is variation according to the conditions. Some representative territory sizes are listed below (all areas are given in square miles):

Dabchick	0.001
Gibbon (group of 4)	0.06
Tawny owl	0.1
Mountain gorilla (group of 17)	6
Golden eagle	27
Tiger	50
African bushman (group of 20)	270

GETTING A TERRITORY...

Acquiring a territory is sometimes a case of first come, first served. Those migratory birds that return first to the breeding grounds are able to stake their claim easily. Latecomers may have to move on to another area or else try to take ground from earlier residents. Bigger, stronger and more vigorous animals have an advantage if it comes to a fight. Males in possession of a territory are often bigger than those who are not. But being territorial takes its toll, whether it is from constant fighting, or simply from constant display or singing. In some species territorial males gradually lose weight and condition and are ousted from their position later in the season.

...AND KEEPING IT

For most territory owners, though, possession is a very potent weapon. Animals usually respect territorial boundaries. If one does stray into a neighbor's ground it rarely remains long if it is challenged. The owner has a psychological advantage and may drive off even a stronger opponent. Away from their own home ground most animals feel insecure. Many are reluctant to cross over the territorial markers laid down by the owners. A pack of wolves hunts over a huge area and is unlikely to see every potential rival that approaches the edges of the territory. By marking the boundaries with strongly scented urine, though, it can keep any would-be intruders away. Animals as diverse as rhinoceroses and mongooses use dung and urine for this purpose.

FIGHTING AND WEAPONS

Two male Northern fur seals square up to one another on a beach in the north Pacific. Neither backs down. Suddenly one lunges forward, striking towards the maned neck of his opponent. The battle begins to rage, each animal trying to inflict enough injury on his opponent to make him give up the fight. For many minutes they struggle in combat. Then one gives in and turns tail, pursued by the winner.

Animals may fight others of their species over territory, food or mates. Even those that are not equipped for fighting may take part in contests that to them are very important. Chameleons move slowly and are not really built for hurting opponents. But they do take part in ferocious contests in which the loser, though largely undamaged, nonetheless appears to be thoroughly cowed and frightened.

WEAPONS

Some animals, though, are equipped with lethal weapons. The big canine teeth of many meat-eaters are as capable of giving a killing bite to one of their own species as they are to a prey animal. Even many plant-eaters have claws or horns that make good weapons. In most cases these are used against a predator only as a last resort when all other means of defense have failed. But plant-eaters are often ready to use their weapons against their own kind.

Some of these weapons are of gigantic size. The tusks of male African elephants, for example, can weigh 110lb each, and the horns of the Siberian ibex can be up to 5ft long. The rapier-like horns of an antelope such as an oryx, or the massive spiral horns of some wild sheep, can cause enormous damage. Even though they possess such lethal weapons, however, many species have developed structures or behavior that, for the sake of survival of the species, minimize the risks of serious fighting while still posing a threat.

DAMAGE LIMITATION

Species like baboons and sea lions, that fight by stabbing and slashing with their canine teeth, have necks and shoulders that are protected by long fur capes or thickened skin. This takes the worst of the blows and protects the internal organs. Some deer also have protective manes on their necks, as do male lions, and during fights they are careful to keep the best protected areas facing the opponent. Bison, which clash head to head, have thick skulls and huge shoulders to absorb the impact.

LOCKED IN COMBAT

Some animal weapons, although they look fearsome, are actually structured to minimize damage. The massive ridged horns of some goats provide

◄The vast yawn of a hippopotamus is a threatening gesture which shows off its main weapons – the huge canine teeth at the front corners of the jaw.

good non-slip surfaces, so that when they crash together they lock rather than slip onto vulnerable parts of the skull. Though sharply pointed and potentially damaging, the branched shape of deer antlers allows them to be used not so much for stabbing but for grappling. Two combatants lock antlers together and push back and forward in a harmless, but effective, trial of strength. Some antelope too have horns that fit together in non-injurious wrestling matches.

THREATS

Despite all the safeguards, occasionally rivals may indeed fight until one is fatally injured. This can happen in some confrontations between male Red deer, but usually, in almost all species, a fight to the death is very much the exception. In a fatal combat even the victor is likely to be hurt and so it is in the species' interest to settle disputes with minimum harm.

Many animals manage to win fights without striking a single blow simply

▲Two massive Southern elephant seals fight for mating territory on a beach. They lunge with open mouths at the neck of an opponent, and may wound deeply. The scars of many former battles are clearly visible on these animals.

▼Contrasting fighting styles Muntjac deer males (1) have very small antlers which are of little use in fighting, but they do have sharp canine teeth that they can use for slashing at an opponent. The klipspringer (2) has short horns, but they are sharply pointed, and can be used for jabbing a rival.

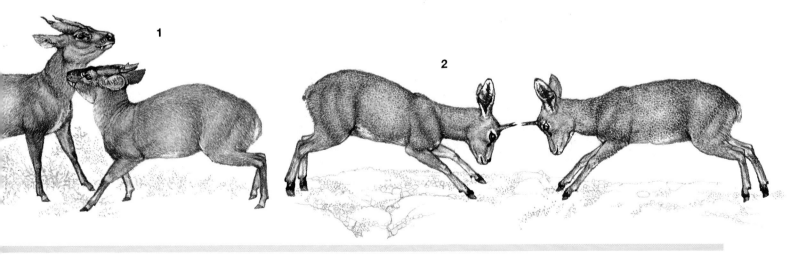

1

2

by showing they are bigger and stronger, thus intimidating a rival. Rival male baboons "yawn" at each other, displaying the ferocious canine teeth. Sometimes they also use vocal threats, and even staring hard is often threatening enough, as it is in many other species. Other ploys used to intimidate include roaring, as in Red deer. Because larger, and therefore stronger, individuals usually have a deeper roar, the use of vocal threats provides a means by which rivals can gauge their relative strengths. Raising the fur to appear larger is also a useful technique that is commonly used by rival dogs and cats. Often antagonists will stand in a way that makes them look as tall as possible.

GIVING IN
To reduce the risk of damage in a fight even further, it is important for the losing animal to acknowledge defeat so that the fighting stops. Sometimes losers just turn and run away but often, especially in species that live in groups, they use a special signal called a submissive posture. A wolf or dog that gives in to another will present its throat to the victor or even roll on to

its back with its legs pointing upwards. Either of these postures makes it very vulnerable. The opponent could then easily bite it but the submissive posture seems to switch off the aggressive feelings of the winner, who seems to be satisfied by this acknowledgement of his superiority.

Losers of monkey fights will cringe with a special scream or turn their rumps to the victor. Again this stops further aggression, and the winner may touch or even groom the loser to cement the new relationship.

SEX AND AGGRESSION
In most species it is the males that have to hold territories or compete for mates. In consequence they are larger and more aggressive than the females. In those species where the males maintain harems of females, as in baboons, elephant seals or goats, the size difference is particularly marked. In a very small number of species, however, this characteristic is reversed. Among the birds, the phalaropes and painted snipes are two groups in which the female has several mates and tends to be larger and more aggressive than the male.

◀Silverbacked jackals fight over a kill. With lips drawn back into a snarl they show sharp teeth, but the fight is more ritual than actual biting.

▼Two Senegal chameleons fight on a branch. The green, puffed-up one is winning, while the other turns pale in acknowledgement of defeat.

COURTSHIP

A male spider arrives at a female's web. He is smaller than she is and moves towards her with caution. A fly lands on the web. Before the female reaches it, the male parcels up the fly in silk strands. He holds it out as a gift to the female. She takes it and begins to feed. While she is busy the male mates with her. This is just one of a number of ways in which spider males go about their dangerous courtships.

Courtship is the behavior that takes place before, during and just after the act of mating. It takes an enormous variety of forms in different groups of animals. At times it is very elaborate, but if it ensures that mating and subsequent breeding both take place successfully, it does its job.

WHY IS COURTSHIP NEEDED?

Courtship can help animals find one another. Because each species has its own pattern of courtship, an animal can identify a potential mate and reject those of other species with the "wrong" pattern. In many animals the mates are initially strangers and courtship can help them become less nervous of one another. Courtship may also trigger an animal's body to complete the process of becoming ready to mate. In some animals, even if all other conditions are satisfactory for mating, eggs mature only after a period of courtship.

LOCATING A MATE

For small animals, especially those species in which individuals live far apart, finding a mate can present great difficulties. Some solve the problem by both sexes congregating at a particular site. Male and female dungflies are attracted to fresh cowpats. Here they meet, mate, and lay their eggs. Some birds have traditional breeding

▲▶**Ways of courting** The male mandrill (*Papio sphinx*) **(1)** is large and brightly patterned to impress the female. A drake mallard (*Anas platyrhynchos*) **(2)** attracts a mate by ritual preening. Courting Black-headed gulls (*Larus ridibundus*) **(3)** face away from one another so as not to look aggressive. A male Sage grouse (*Centrocercus urophasianus*) **(4)** displays to the smaller females on a communal mating site.

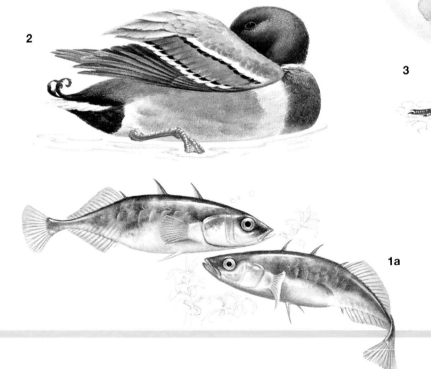

grounds. Sage grouse, for example, return each year to the same sites, called leks, where the males display to attract onlooking females to mate.

Amphibians such as toads and newts also return to traditional sites to breed, typically the ponds in which they themselves hatched. Turtles and seals return year after year to the same breeding beaches, sometimes many miles from their usual haunts.

ADVERTISING FOR A MATE

Birds are not the only animals capable of attracting a mate by singing. In many frogs and insects the males make calls that can be heard over hundreds of yards. The voices of frogs are often amplified by inflatable sacs in the throat. Insects such as grasshoppers and crickets produce sounds by stridulation – rubbing one part of the body against another. Mole crickets call from the safety of a burrow which is specially shaped to increase the sound-level.

Among animals that use chirps in courtship, such as grasshoppers and frogs, the sound receptors ("ears") of the females are often sensitive only to the particular frequencies used by males of their own species. They may be effectively deaf to sounds, however loud or numerous, made by other kinds of animal.

Some animals even use flashing lights to attract a mate. Fireflies are beetles that are active at night. They have light-producing organs. Males fly around making distinctive sequences of flashes. Females stay on the ground but respond to males of their own species by flashing back. The wingless female glow-worm, a European beetle, produces a greenish-blue light from the underside of its abdomen. At dusk it sits in the grass with its tail turned up and light on to attract a winged male to mate. Some of the deep sea fishes and squids also have light organs that can be used for identification or attraction.

◄► Courtship among fish and amphibians The male stickleback (*Gasterosteus aculeatus*) (1a), with red belly, dances in front of a female. A male European tree frog (*Hyla arborea*) (2a) calls by using an enlarged vocal sac.

4

2a

SIGNALING READINESS

In social animals, where locating a potential mate is not so much a problem, it may be useful nonetheless for females to use signals that show they are ready for mating. In baboons, for example, the female has an area of skin on her rump that swells and reddens when she is in breeding condition. Female chimpanzees also have sexual swellings to show their readiness to mate.

REDUCING AGGRESSION

For mating to take place it may be necessary to defuse the normal wariness or aggression between two animals. Often the female is the smaller, weaker sex, and the male is careful not to alarm her. In leopards the male gently nuzzles and caresses the female as they get to know one another. In giraffes the male rubs the neck of a female in order to reassure her during courtship.

Courting birds are also careful to avoid signaling aggression and may conspicuously look away from a prospective partner rather than risk

► Two Western grebes court by running on the water. Ritualized sequences like this are typical of bird courtship.

▼ The Great crested grebe has some of the most elaborate courtship displays. Headshaking with crests raised (1). One dives, while the other puffs up in display (2). One displays, the other rises out of the water (3). Dancing upright and showing nest material to each other (4).

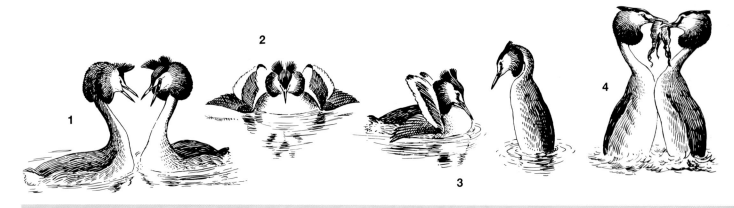

1

2

3

4

giving what could be interpreted as a hostile stare. One or both partners may take up a submissive posture to avoid provoking aggression.

The members of a pair of courting animals may initially be in a state of internal conflict, both perhaps torn between mating, fighting or running away. It is not surprising that courtship is often stopped in its early stages.

DISPLACED BEHAVIOR
When animals are in such a state of conflict some strange, apparently irrelevant, behavior can occur. A courting male will suddenly break off to scratch or preen. These so-called displacement activities can be seen in birds such as ducks. In this group these actions have actually become ritualized and fixed so that they now form part of the display.

During the courtship of mallard ducks the male performs a display in which he turns his head as though to preen a distinctively colored patch of feathers on the wing, but instead merely touches it.

SUICIDE MISSIONS
For the males of a few kinds of animal, courtship can be a very dangerous activity. In spiders the female is usually larger than the male, sometimes very

much so. A female spider is likely to regard a smaller one as potential dinner, so the males have a variety of courtship techniques to help them overcome this problem. Among the web-spinners males may pluck and vibrate the threads of the female's web in a pattern that she recognizes as that of a mate rather than a catch. Among the wolf spiders, that have no web, the male may display by waving his mouthparts and drumming them on the ground. Other spiders perform ritualized dances or leg-wavings. The displays quieten a female long enough for mating to take place, but it is wise for the male to leave straight after. By using these ploys few get eaten.

Female Praying mantises too are larger than the males. In these insects the male's courtship technique is not always good enough for him to avoid being eaten by his mate, but a male may be able to complete mating by reflex actions even after the female has bitten off his head.

RITUAL CHASES
The courtship behavior of several mammals can be seen as an extension of the male chasing the female. The courtship of the hare, in which chases are interrupted by ritual boxing matches and leaps, is a good example.

▲ In the male Domestic fowl (1) and in the Common pheasant (2) the male displays his bright colors to the female during courtship. In other pheasants, such as the impeyan (3) and the peacock-pheasant (4), a spreading tail is added to the display. In the peafowl (5) the male spreads a huge tail covered with dazzling eye markings to attract and impress the female.

In some antelopes, too, courtship is ritualized pursuit, the male parading stiff-legged after the female, sometimes flapping his ears or lifting his neck as added elements of attraction in the display.

BIZARRE RITES
Some of the oddest formalized displays are found among the birds. Many of them are fairly simple to understand. That of a finch dancing

up and down in front of his hen with a grass stalk in his beak can be seen as having a direct connection with nestbuilding. On the other hand, though a bird-of-paradise hanging upside down and showing off the brilliant collection of feathers on his under-side to a hen is undoubtedly very spectacular, it is not so easy to understand how such a display, and the equipment for it, ever arose.

It may be a case of "the bigger the better." This would account for the peacock's tail train which can be erected into a splendidly eyecatching display. But there must be a point when such highly over-developed equipment becomes a disadvantage in everyday life. Usually it is hard to show whether females do actually prefer the biggest displays, but this has been shown to be the case with East African widowbirds. In this species the males have long black ribbon-like tails. In an experiment, those of some males were cut short and the removed sections were used to lengthen the tails of other males. These "extra good" males attracted more females than the normal widowbirds.

CORRECTLY TIMED

One of the most important purposes of courtship is to synchronize the behavior of male and female so that they are ready for breeding in the same place, at the same time, and in the right position. This may be especially important for the species which simply shed eggs and sperm

▼A male giraffe, having won the right to mate with the females in a herd, proceeds to court one of them. The males engage in mock fights to determine which is the most dominant.

into the water, such as many fishes. The dance of the sticklebacks or the maneuvers of salmon on the stream bed ensure that egg and sperm release is simultaneous.

FINAL PREPARATIONS

Some animals, including humans and monkeys, produce eggs in regular cycles. But many others come into breeding condition for only a short period during the year. Temperature, daylength, abundance of food and other factors in the surroundings may influence when this takes place. But the females may not actually produce eggs until very precise conditions are met. For example, Green lizards do not produce mature eggs unless males display to them first. Female canaries come into breeding condition much more quickly if they hear the song of a male. Female pigeons too need the bowing and cooing display of the male before they can produce eggs. Some animal species, such as the stoat even need to mate before they are able to produce eggs.

▲ **Courtship in newts and salamanders**
Special chemicals made by the males' chin glands stimulate the females to position themselves for mating. In the Two-lined salamander (*Eurycea bislineata*) (1) the male covers the female's neck with secretions, then scratches her skin with sharp teeth (1a). The male Jordan's salamander (*Plethodon jordani*) (2) leads the female, often turning to slap his gland against her snout. In the Redbelly newt (*Taricha rivularis*) (3) the male rubs his gland on the female's snout. The male Smooth newt (*Triturus vulgaris*) (4) uses his long tail to waft odors secreted from his glands towards a nearby female.

PARENTS AND YOUNG

A mother rat has been out looking for food for herself. Now she is returning to feed her babies in their nest. They are newborn and need her milk at regular intervals. As she nears the nest she hears a high-pitched squeaking. One of the babies, still so young it can only wriggle, has tumbled from the warmth of the nest. Immediately she goes to pick it up, then returns to the nest and suckles all the babies.

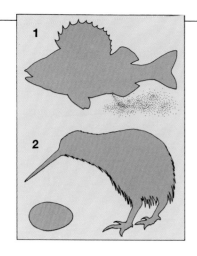

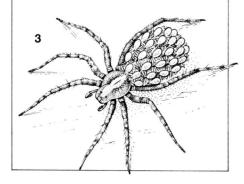

The perch (1) takes no care of its eggs. It may lay 200,000 of them each ½in across. The kiwi (2) lays the largest egg for its size of any bird: a 4lb female lays an egg 5in long weighing 1lb. The wolf spider female (3) carries young on her back for a few days after they hatch. Many scorpions also protect their young like this.

We humans are mammals and tend to assume that parents will look after their babies. But most members of the animal kingdom take no care at all of their offspring. They make up for this apparent neglect by producing such large numbers of eggs that even though most will die before maturity, at least a few will survive to carry on the species. Some of the most successful animals, however, are those that invest effort in caring for their young. They may produce fewer offspring, but each one stands a greater chance of becoming an adult.

EGG CARE

Some animals put a large amount of yolk into their eggs to serve as food for the young during their early development. When fish fry hatch from the egg they still carry the yolk sac with them and can live on this for days. The yolk is very large in the eggs of reptiles such as crocodiles and turtles, and of course in birds' eggs.

A typical fish or amphibian takes little notice of its eggs. A reptile may take care to bury them in an appropriate place, but only a tiny number guard their nests. Only in birds do the parents typically sit on the eggs to incubate them, and then spend some time feeding the young and keeping them warm after they hatch. But in many other animal groups there are some species that, exceptionally, tend their eggs. Some millipedes guard them and there are spiders that weave a special web for eggs and hatchlings to live in. Other spiders, and many scorpions, carry their young for a time after they hatch.

CARING FISH

Among the fishes, some cichlids excavate a nest hollow and then guard the eggs laid in it. Others, like the Egyptian mouthbrooder, gather the eggs into their mouths to protect them until they hatch. This may take 1 to 2 weeks, during which time the mother cannot feed. Some cichlids protect the young after they hatch, taking them into the mouth when danger threatens.

GIVING BIRTH

Although some lizards and snakes bear so-called live young, they simply retain their eggs inside their bodies until it is time for hatching. During this time the embryo feeds only on the yolk in the egg. Some fishes, such as guppies and some sharks, have similar "live births." All these animals ignore their offspring after they are born.

▶ A cuckoo chick stimulates the parental behavior of its foster parent, which in this case is a Reed warbler.

▼ A baby Olive baboon sucks milk from its mother. Only mammals feed their babies in this way.

It is among the mammals that the most advanced system of birth and baby care is found. A mammal grows inside its mother's body, nourished through the placenta, a structure that brings it in close contact with the mother's blood system. When it has developed enough to lead a more independent life, it is born. The mother continues to feed the baby on milk produced by areas of special skin glands, and typically takes great care of the young, cleaning it, protecting it and keeping it warm.

FEEDING BABIES

Mammal mothers need a huge amount of energy to produce their milk. A Bank vole has to eat twice as much as usual when she is feeding young. A Gray seal mother feeds her baby for less than 3 weeks but in this time the pup may put on over 65lb. The mother loses much more than this, as she has no chance to feed during the suckling period.

Bird parents must gather food for their young, and they too expend a lot

▲A lion cub takes its first solid meal. The process of weaning – changing from a diet of milk to adult food – is one which every baby mammal must go through.

►Babies of mammals such as the Brown rat are born blind, naked and helpless. The mother must take care of all their needs until they can leave the nest.

▼A Chinstrap penguin, feeding its chick with krill brought back from the sea, fights off scavenging sheathbills. Most birds fiercely protect their young.

In others, however, the number may be different. For animals that invest a lot of care in their young, such as elephants, monkeys or humans, the usual number of offspring they raise at a time is just one.

RECOGNIZING BABY
Baby mammals, and birds too, have characteristics which seem to make them attractive to adults. They have rounder faces and bigger eyes than adults, and this seems to stimulate caring behavior. Occasionally they may be differently colored too, as in many birds and monkeys. Baby baboons are black and pink, for example, whereas the adults are olive. Such babies may be attractive not only to their mothers, but also, to other adult and adolescent females, who may try to pick them up.

BONDING
In some species frequent separation between mother and her young is routine. Nestling birds or rats get used to parents disappearing and returning. In other species the young become quite distressed if they are separated from their mother. This might be the case even in species whose young seem to be less reliant on a parent in that they move around soon after birth, such as goslings and ducklings, or sheep and antelopes. But such offspring form a close bond with the mother. When a sheep is born its mother cleans and smells it. After this mother and offspring recognize each other and the parent sheep will not accept a lamb with a different smell. If they are separated the lamb bleats in distress until the ewe, recognizing its offspring's cries, finds it again.

In monkeys too a baby will cry for its mother if left behind. Usually this results in her return. If the mother does not come back for some reason the baby may pine and die, even if other members of the group are willing to look after it.

of energy in the process. Many birds must feed their young as often as ten times an hour throughout the day to satisfy the nestlings' appetites.

Some invertebrates also take care of the food needs of their offspring but in less demanding ways. Butterflies, moths and many other insects lay their eggs on plants which will be food for the larvae. Some solitary wasps lay their eggs in a burrow, having first filled it with another insect. Alive but unable to move because it has been paralyzed by the wasp's sting, the insect will become fresh food for the mass of grubs when they hatch.

HOW BIG A FAMILY?
In animals that care for their young there is a limit to the number that can be raised successfully. Female swifts usually lay three eggs in a clutch. Why not lay more? Swifts that were given artificially large broods had great difficulty finding enough food for all the young, and as a result many died. On average, three babies seems to be the optimum number for this species.

FAMILY LIFE

It is a sunny day in summer. Deep in a wood three fox cubs are playing near a burrow. Their mother sits above them, keeping watch. A male fox comes trotting up the valley with a rabbit in his mouth. He greets the vixen. She feeds while the father takes his turn watching the cubs. Then the pair rest in the Sun, still watchful, and the tired cubs sleep snuggled up to them.

Mammals such as the beaver and the gibbons are unusual in that they form families consisting of one male, one female and their young. This arrangement is common in birds too, but for most animals that take care of their young the family is quite a different kind of unit.

A MOTHER'S WORK
In many mammals, from rodents to tigers and bears, the male and female have very little more to do with one another after they have mated. In fact, in species such as the tiger it is safer for the young if they do not see their father, because he is as likely to attack them as help with their upbringing.

Even in those species where males and females live together in a herd for much of the time, such as the Black-buck antelope, the males never show any interest in the young. All care is by the mother. In such cases the family unit is simply a mother and her current young.

LONG-TERM FAMILIES
The chimpanzee is one of the animals whose young stay with their mother for some years. Young males may be up to 7 or 8 years old before they become independent. Young females

sometimes stay even longer and may still move around with their mother when they are adult and have babies of their own to look after.

In the African elephant, the adult males are often solitary, but females and young live in groups that are extended families. Cow elephants commonly stay with their mother from the time they are born until she dies. As cows are able to breed at 12 years old and live to be 60, an elephant can spend up to 50 years in a stable family unit.

HELPING MOTHER
In those families that stay together for long periods a mother often gets help from older young in caring for the smallest one in the family. Elephant females may care for their young relatives, and the same is also true of the Rhesus monkey and all meerkats, where babies are groomed, watched over or carried by older sisters. In a few birds, such as the House martin, older young help in feeding nestlings.

BIRD FAMILIES
The young of many birds are raised in a nest, and even after they have all

▶ **Family arrangements** More than one female ostrich (*Struthio camelus*) **(1)** may lay her eggs in the nest scrape made by a male, but a single pair do the work of incubation and early chick care. In the Cotton-top tamarin (*Sanguinus oedipus*) **(2)** the older offspring help their parents look after the twin babies. Savannah baboons (*Papio cynocephalus*) **(3)** live in troops of several family groups.

▶ The inhabitants of a Black-tailed prairie dog burrow will all be members of the same family group.

▶**Sex differences** Males and females are often of a similar size in species, like the Moloch gibbon (*Hylobates moloch*) **(1)**, in which a male mates with a single female. When males mate with many females there is often a size difference between the sexes, as in the Northern elephant seal (*Mirounga anguistirostris*) **(2)**, the capercaillie (*Tetrao urogallus*) **(3)** and the Black howler monkey (*Alouatta caraya*) **(4)**. The male is much larger.

◀A gorilla group is based on a large family consisting of one fully adult silver-backed male together with several females and their young.

fledged parents help them for a while by providing food. Soon, however, the families break up and the young go their own way. Some of the best examples of birds that move around as families can be found among those that leave the nest soon after hatching. Ducklings keep together with their mother, following her wherever they can. This behavior is very strongly developed because it increases the young's chances of finding food and avoiding enemies.

Baby ostriches are obviously much smaller and more vulnerable than the adults, though they can walk and run at a very early age. At this stage the parents protectively shepherd them about, fiercely guarding them from predators. Later, several groups of young from different parents come together and are tended by one or two adults as though they were all members of one very large family.

WHEN DAD IS MUM

In the other large, flightless birds – emu, rhea, and cassowary – it is the job of the male to incubate the eggs. Unusually, the female plays no further part after laying them. The male also protects and moves about with the young after they hatch. Male emus and rheas with chicks are very fierce defenders of their family. Emu fathers look after the young for up to about 7 months and cassowary families stay together for as long as a year.

HITCHING A LIFT

Some animal mothers carry their young about if there is a hint of danger. A nursing rat, if disturbed, will move to another nest, carrying its babies one by one in its mouth. Many carnivores, from weasels to lions, also carry their young in this way.

But some babies are carried about by the mother most of the time,

making the family a mobile one. A koala mother carries her baby on her back once it has left the pouch. Opossums too carry their babies on their backs. Very young baboons and chimpanzees cling firmly under their mother's belly as she walks on all fours, but when they are older they ride on her back, jockey-fashion.

GROWING UP

As young animals grow older and their abilities develop, so they need less attention from their parents. There comes a time when they leave their families or are driven from them. The parents may need to concentrate on breeding again, or simply on winter survival.

In many meat-eaters the period of care in the family can be quite long because hunting is a difficult way of obtaining food and learning how to do it takes time. The mother has to show the young suitable prey and teach them how to catch it.

For monkeys and apes the process of becoming independent is often very gradual even though it may begin at an early stage. When their babies are as young as 2 weeks, mother baboons play games in which they place the youngsters on the ground, walk away a few paces, then turn back with a gesture of reassurance. Later the mothers tend to leave the babies more often and will reject many of their attempts to suckle. Even when they no longer feed from her, the young may still be cuddled by the mother. Eventually the adult's attention turns to mating and bringing up another baby. She becomes quite intolerant of older young being close to her for much of the time, but by now they are no longer physically or emotionally dependent on her.

GROUPS AND TROOPS

A big troop of baboons moves across the savannah. Around the edges are alert young males, the eyes and ears of the group. Within this ring of guards are the females and their young. A huge adult male, the father of many of the babies, stays in the middle of the troop, close to the adult females. All the animals in the group know all the others, and their place in the troop.

Many animal species live in groups: the hives of bees, the schools of fishes, the herds of deer, the flocks of birds. Some groups form simply because the food is concentrated in a small area where individuals must congregate in order to feed. The individuals in a large flock of starlings or within a big shoal of sardines do not know one another and have no special roles. But many groups are not just masses of independent individuals. Especially in social insects and the mammals, animals which show the most highly developed instances of group-living, different individuals may have their separate roles. This increases the efficiency of the group's activities.

INSECT SOCIETIES

Group living is practiced by two main types of insect: the termites, and some of the bees, wasps and ants. In the bumblebee a fertilized female survives the winter. In the spring she makes an underground nest and raises young. The next generation join her in care of young and nest. Here the society is fairly simple and lasts only the one season. In some social wasps and bees it is much more complex and sometimes, as in the honeybee, it is long-lasting.

In a honeybee hive there is only one fertile female, the queen. Other females are workers and do not reproduce. They have four main duties which they perform in sequence as they get older. First they clean cells; then they build combs and feed larvae; next they receive nectar and pollen, remove debris and guard the hive; finally they go out foraging. The queen produces a special chemical, called a pheromone, that is spread through the colony by the workers as they communicate by touching antennae. The pheromone stops the production of any new queens. If the queen dies, or the hive becomes very big and the pheromone too thinly spread, then the workers' behavior

is changed. They take some of the queen's eggs and start to rear them in the special way that will produce new queens. One new queen takes over the hive and the old one leaves, taking some of the workers with her, to form a new colony.

A termite colony has a king and queen at its center. There is a worker caste, made up of "immature" termites whose development has been prevented, and a soldier caste which defends the colony. Soldiers have large heads and either big jaws to bite with or a snout which can shoot sticky, poisonous substances. Once again there is a division of tasks and regulation of individual behavior.

INSECT-LIKE MAMMAL

Only one species of mammal is known to run a caste system with an insect-like division of labor. This is the strange Naked mole-rat, an almost hairless species from east Africa. It lives in an underground colony with a tunnel system up to as much as 2mi long. At the heart is a nest chamber where the only breeding female produces her 40 or more pups a year. Successive litters become the workers that dig tunnels and find food. Some grow larger than others and seem to

▲ ▶ Some animals, like the Muntjac deer from Asia, spend nearly all their lives alone. Others live permanently in groups or, like this huge herd of Subantarctic fur seals, for part of every year.

become a guard caste. Only if the breeding female dies will another develop the ability to reproduce.

WHY FORM GROUPS?

Living in a group can help animals to avoid predators, to find a mate and rear offspring more efficiently, or to find food more effectively. White-fronted geese in a small flock spend more of their time looking out for predators than do those in a large one. The bigger the flock, the more time there is to devote to feeding.

It may be that an animal in a group also does better at finding food. But there can be some disadvantages to group living as well. Food may well be found more easily, but individuals may get less because they have to share with others. Competition for valuable resources within a group is not uncommon. Chickens jostle for grains of wheat, and baboons squabble over the best and safest ledges on which to sleep.

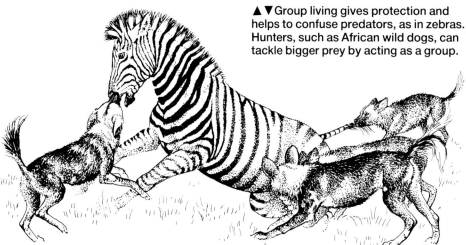

▲▼Group living gives protection and helps to confuse predators, as in zebras. Hunters, such as African wild dogs, can tackle bigger prey by acting as a group.

SORTED INTO ORDER

In order to minimize constant fighting, many groups develop a ranking system so that individuals "know their place." This was first observed in chickens and the arrangement is therefore often known as a "pecking order." When a number of hens first meet they fight over which will have precedence. One emerges as the most dominant (the boss) and it will peck at all the others and push them aside. The next strongest will give way to the boss but will push the others around; and so on down to the last hen that gets chased by all the others. Once the birds have learnt their place in the group there may be very little actual fighting. Pecking orders (also known as dominance hierarchies) are found in mammals as well as in birds. There are some obvious advantages to being high in the pecking order, such as having the first choice of food or mates. High ranking animals often have more success at breeding than do lower ones.

FOLLOW MY LEADER

Animals living in a group must have a way of staying together. The group may have a leader that the others all follow. This is clearly the arrangement among cattle and sheep. In elephants and lions an adult male may be the biggest and strongest animal in the group at any one time, but he often remains aloof from all of the other members, who usually follow the lead of an old, experienced female.

At breeding time some groups are kept together by the adult male. A Red deer stag rounds up any of his females that try to stray and so maintains the integrity of the group. The same is true of baboons such as the Hamadryas, or some kinds of fur seal which, by possessively herding their females, manage to create some semblance of order out of the apparent chaos of a teeming breeding beach.

Some of the most spectacular examples of groups keeping together are provided by big shoals of fishes. Hundreds or thousands of individuals swim together side by side. They turn, accelerate or slow down, all in perfect unison. Keeping together is partly a matter of watching one's neighbors but, surprisingly, fishes may do almost as well with their eyes covered. The lateral line that runs down the side of the animal is a sense organ that can feel disturbances in the water, including those made by other fishes. This information is enough to keep a fish in a shoal "on station."

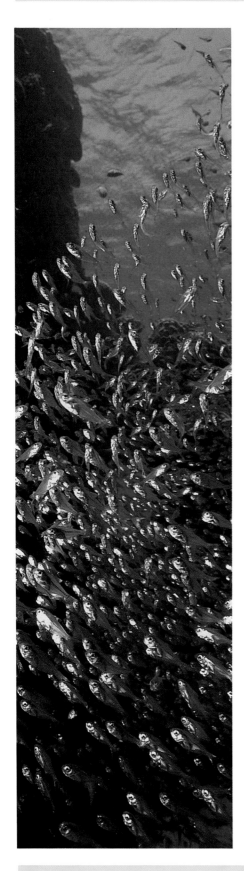

◀ Many fishes form large shoals in which individuals seem to act in perfect unison. As the fishes twist and turn their silvery flashes and the shoal's changing shape probably serve to confuse enemies.

GROOMING COUNTS

Grooming can be an important factor in keeping some kinds of group together. Many monkeys and apes spend a large part of their "leisure" time picking through one another's fur. They spend far more time on this than would be necessary for simply removing dirt and parasites. The explanation seems to be that this is an activity which gives pleasure to both groomer and the animal being groomed. The latter may find the experience so relaxing that it actually goes off to sleep. This apparently pleasurable activity has become a bond that helps keep the group together. Grooming may also be used to pacify another animal after a squabble, or to establish a friendly relationship between two strangers. Mutual grooming has been observed in many other species, ranging from horses to lovebirds.

CHANGING GROUPS

Although some animals never leave the same group, many individuals

do change groups in their lifetime. Adolescent male lions are driven out by the adult males. These outcasts usually join an all-male bachelor group. Young male antelope and deer also commonly spend some time in a male herd until they are sufficiently old and strong to battle for females. Bachelor herds like these are usually relaxed about letting new members join. The same is not true, however, if a young male is rash enough to try joining a breeding group.

▼Spinner dolphins ride a bow wave. These animals live in social groups of up to 100 during the day but spread out at night to feed. They may join together in different groups next day.

▲A Kloss gibbon calls from a branch, while his mate and baby search for food. These animals live in small and stable family groups. A distant male (top left) answers, his family clustered near him.

▼Society life In social animals such as Hamadryas baboons each individual, as it matures, finds its place through activities such as infant play (1) and exploring (2), grooming (3), foraging (4) and aggressive encounters (5).

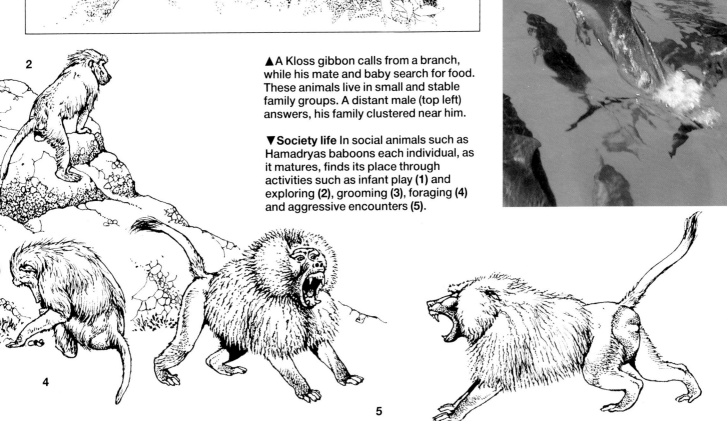

UNSELFISH BEHAVIOR

A fox prowls near the shore through a colony of nesting plovers. One of the birds begins to shuffle along the ground in front of the fox, with its wing held out as though it is injured. The fox notices the bird and begins to follow it, for it may be easy prey. The bird allows the fox to get quite close before making its escape. It has done its job of leading the fox away from its chicks.

Much of the behavior we all see in animals can be regarded as "selfish," in the sense that it seems to be designed to help the individual survive and do as well as possible for itself, even if this is at the expense of others of its own kind. But in some animals we see examples of behavior which seems unselfish in that it appears to bring no immediate reward to the individual

performing it. Indeed, it may bring the animal discomfort or even death. But it must always be remembered that such self-sacrifice may help others, and in nature the survival of the species is considerably more important than the survival of the individual.

HEROIC PARENTS

Many animals which normally avoid trouble will turn and fight enemies in defense of their young. Blackbirds usually call in alarm and flee at the sight of a cat; but when they have young nearby they will pursue the cat and dive at it, even though this may mean endangering themselves.

There are many other examples where parental devotion to duty is of obvious use to the offspring but is dangerous or debilitating for the parent. The Emperor penguin's care

▲ A single sentinel stands guard in an exposed position to warn a Long-tailed marmot colony of approaching danger.

▼ A living zip. Green tree ant workers show selfless service as they draw two sides of a leaf together to form a nest.

of its egg is a spectacular case. The father stands through 6 weeks of the Antarctic winter incubating the egg on his feet. He must regularly endure strong winds and blizzards in temperatures as low as −40°F. He cannot feed during this time and loses an enormous amount of weight. Not until the egg hatches and his mate returns from the sea to take over can he make his way over the ice for up to 60mi to reach the sea and find food. This behavior may well be advantageous to the species as a whole in that it enables the Emperor penguin pairs to breed successfully almost every year, but it is a tremendous ordeal to the males as individuals.

INSECT SACRIFICE
Social insects provide many instances where the individual sacrifices itself to

▼A meerkat acts as a babysitter to its young brothers and sisters while their mother hunts with the pack.

the colony. When a worker honeybee stings an intruder, the barbed sting is often torn out of the defender's body, leaving it fatally injured. The bee dies but its death is useful to the hive.

Ant workers too fight fiercely in defense of their colony and many die, even though, as individuals, they could have avoided the danger. Some also make "living bridges" so that other workers may cross water or other obstacles. Some of those that form the bridge may perish.

MAKING ALLIANCES
Sometimes mammals form alliances in which one is apparently acting unselfishly on behalf of another. A

male baboon may enlist the aid of another to distract a big male away from a female that is ready to mate. The first one sneaks in to grab the female, while the other may have nothing to show for helping out except the discomfort of a fight. But often these alliances seem to work on a "you scratch my back, I'll scratch yours" basis. The one who gives the favor may expect one back later.

▼Banded mongooses will aid their companions. A pack can chase off a jackal. A Martial eagle was once seen to catch a mongoose and carry it to the fork of a tree . The other mongooses climbed the tree and lunged at the eagle, which dropped its catch unhurt.

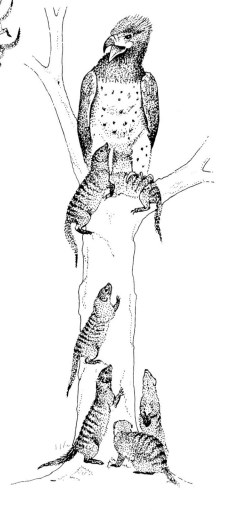

INSTINCT AND LEARNING

A brood of ducklings has recently hatched from their eggs. Their mother is close by. Soon they are standing and able to move. The mother duck moves away from the nest. Automatically the little ducklings follow after her.

There are some things that an animal must be able to do early in life, before it has had a chance to learn. For those birds that leave the nest almost immediately after hatching, the ability to follow mother is essential because they need her protection and help in finding food. These birds are "programmed" so that they follow the first large moving object they see after hatching. This is known as "imprinting." In the natural state this will be mother. Once they have "recognized" their mother they will readily follow her, but they will react to other large animals with suspicion or fright. This kind of inbuilt response is known as instinctive behavior. It seems to be passed on from generation to generation, inherited in much the same way as physical characteristics such as hair color or body size.

STARTER PACK

Instinct provides a kind of starter pack that puts an animal on the right track when it is beginning life. The nuzzling of a baby mammal, looking for a teat to suck, is instinctive. It does not need to be taught that this is the way of finding its first food.

Those baby birds that stay for some time in the nest usually have a strong begging instinct. When a parent lands by the nest a nestling raises its head and opens wide its mouth. Often the inside of a young bird's mouth is colored or patterned in a way that switches on the parent's instinct to put food into it. The system works automatically.

OTHER INSTINCTS

Other aspects of animal behavior seem in part to be governed by inbuilt reactions. For example, the presence of eggs in its nest will trigger a strong brooding action in a parent bird, even if it has not laid them.

Several surprisingly complicated actions are carried out instinctively. Birds do not have to learn how to build their nests, however intricate these may be – when the time comes, they simply gather material and do it.

INSTINCTIVELY WRONG

One drawback to fixed, inbuilt patterns of behavior is that they can sometimes be triggered by signals which are not genuine. For example, the feeding instinct of a parent bird can be stimulated by even a crude model of a nestling's gaping mouth.

Many ground-nesting birds have the instinct to pull dislodged eggs back into the nest. If they are supplied with fake eggs they will do the same. For some birds it seems that the bigger the egg, the more determined is the recovery behavior. Most birds can

▼▶ How to get a meal. A Laughing gull chick (below) aims a "begging peck" at the parent's beak **(1)**. It grasps the beak and pulls it downward **(2)**. The parent then regurgitates food **(3)**. The chick eats the food with a "feeding peck" **(4)**. In the Great black-backed gull (right) the chick begs for food by pecking at the parent's beak, aiming at the red spot on the tip.

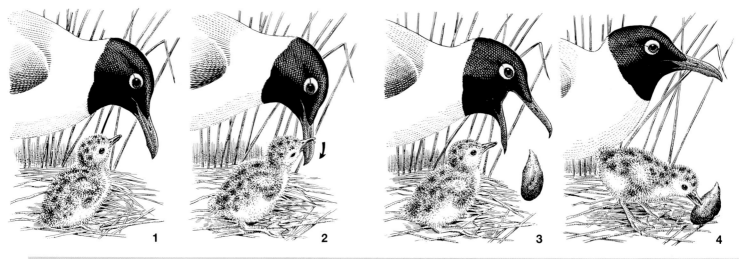

1   2   3   4

be deceived into retrieving and trying to sit on absurdly large eggs.

The mother-following instinct of ducklings and goslings can also fail. If the parent is absent when the eggs hatch, some other nearby animal or object may be adopted as a "mother."

INSTINCTS GONE CUCKOO

Most of these examples of instincts going wrong are perhaps likely only under experimental conditions, but sometimes similar "mistakes" do occur in the wild. Cuckoos make use of just such opportunities. A cuckoo lays an egg in the nest of another kind of bird. Unaware, the foster-parents brood the egg along with their own.

When the young cuckoo hatches it throws all the other eggs or newly hatched young out of the nest. Seemingly oblivious to everything but the young cuckoo's gaping mouth, the foster-parents instinctively feed it, even though it grows to be far bigger than they are (see page 61).

▲These goslings never saw their true mother, but have become imprinted on the dog. They accept it as "mother" and follow wherever it goes.

▼At first this young cheetah played with the gazelle fawn it found. Then it recognized the fawn as food and proceeded to kill it.

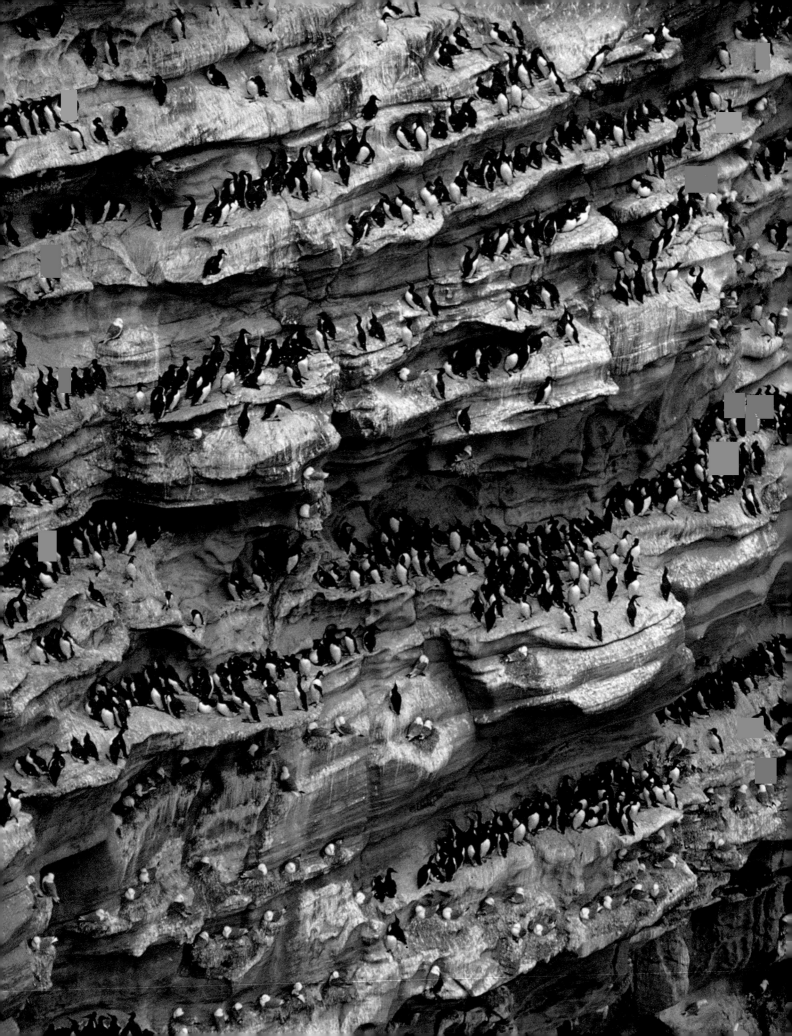

IS LEARNING IMPORTANT?

Over the years there has been a lot of argument about whether instinctive patterns of behavior take on more importance in an animal's life than learned ones. For most animals, of course, the truth is that both instinct and learning shape what they do. Often it seems that instinct provides a basic pattern of behavior, to which learning adds the finishing touches.

A good example of this is the way that young gulls peck at their parents' beaks to get them to regurgitate food. The Herring gull's beak is yellow with a red spot on it, and the chick directs its peck at the red spot. The pecking starts very early in life, and chicks a few days old will peck only at their parent's beaks, or at model beaks very like the real thing.

Does this mean that the chicks hatch with an instinct to peck at the red spot? The answer appears to be no. Careful experiments have shown that newly hatched chicks will peck at all sorts of things, though a rod or beak shape, and red colors, do seem to be preferred. After a few days of real feeding experience, however, they lose all interest in pecking at anything that does not resemble their parents' beak shape and color precisely. So it seems that they are born with an instinct to peck at roughly the right things, but it takes a little time for them to learn where the food really does come from.

INHERITING BEHAVIOR

Important though learning may be, there is no denying that inheritance does influence behavior in many ways. Two strains of otherwise similar laboratory mice may show constant differences in behavior. One strain may be placid and docile, the other jumpy and nervous.

◀Recognition is vital among crowded guillemots. Chicks and parents learn each other's voices as they call through the cracked shell of the hatching egg.

To investigate the connection, we can choose a particular behavioral characteristic and try breeding for it. If rats that are clever at finding their way in a maze are mated to others that are similarly quick, their offspring tend to be bright. Mentally slow rats bred together produce slow offspring. If we can produce a line of bright or dull rats in this way, it shows that behavioral traits can be inherited.

SINGING LESSONS

In many birds it seems that learning puts the finishing touches to an instinctive song. If newly hatched male chaffinches are reared alone they eventually develop a rudimentary form of the normal song. Only after hearing other chaffinches can they imitate and learn the finer note sequences and flourishes of the full version. So precise is this learning by imitation that all the male chaffinches in a particular woodland have very similar songs. Those in another wood may be slightly different. This is similar to the way in which humans

▲A Golden-mantled squirrel scratches its neck. Such scratching is a reflex action that does not need to be learned.

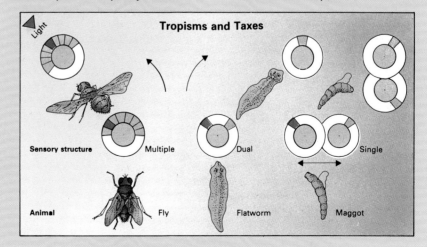

▼Simple instinctive reactions can steer an animal in the required direction. The fly's multi-faceted eyes can pick out the brightest area and allow the fly to move towards it. But even the pair of simple eyes of a flatworm let it compare the light level on each side so that it can select the darker one to move towards. Even a single receptor, moved from side to side as on the maggot's head, can enable such comparisons to be made.

Tropisms and Taxes

Light

Sensory structure — Multiple — Dual — Single

Animal — Fly — Flatworm — Maggot

acquire accents. People from say, Birmingham, all talk alike, and have a different accent to those that live in Dallas or Boston.

Not all species of bird develop their songs in the same way. Some copy less accurately and show more improvisation than others. In most cases young birds seem to recognize instinctively the song of their own species and will copy only that one. A few species, though, will imitate other bird songs, or even other types of sound. Parrots are well known mimics of many sounds, from ringing telephones to human speech. Starlings and mynahs also produce a very wide range of copied sounds, and the mockingbird of North America is famous for its imitations. But the prize probably goes to the male European Marsh warbler which can imitate, on average, 76 other species that live in its nesting and wintering range. What use this ability is, if any, is a mystery.

LEARNING

During a lifetime a human takes in a vast amount of information. We learn some things consciously and others without realizing it. Other animals too learn many things as they experience them and as the need arises. A tame cat will learn how to use a cat flap and when to come for food. A foraging bird will learn that if it is not to be stung or poisoned it should avoid yellow-and-black insects. The instinctive behavior patterns that have been passed on from one generation to the next are modified by the animal as it learns about the particular environment in which it lives.

GETTING USED TO THINGS

One of the simplest and commonest forms of learning is known as "habituation." It is the learning process by which an animal learns to ignore things that are of no particular importance to it. An animal foraging under a tree may at first duck or freeze when

▲A young chimpanzee fishes for termites by inserting a carefully prepared twig into their nest. This skill is learned through careful observation of adults.

▶If they have to, most cats and dogs can learn to open doors. The learning involved may be little more than a fairly random trial-and-error process.

the shadow of a branch, moving in the wind, falls on it. But as this happens again and again the animal realizes there is no danger and carries on foraging, ignoring the moving branch from then on.

TRY IT AND SEE

Animals learn about things that are useful to them, such as the location of food or water, by what is known as "trial-and-error" learning. An animal tries many things, but learns to repeat only those actions that bring a good result. This kind of learning plays an important part in the life of many species, including humans. A young jackdaw may start to build its nest with many kinds of material. It may even try to use tin cans, or pieces of glass and wire. It soon discovers that these make a nest uncomfortable, and finally avoids them in favor of better materials such as twigs and grasses.

Animals also show "avoidance learning." Rats are suspicious of new food in their area and initially eat only a very small amount. If it is poisoned bait the tiny quantity does not kill them but, through feeling ill, they learn to avoid any further contact with the source of discomfort. This learning ability makes controlling these pests very difficult.

INSIGHT

When someone thinks about a problem, then suddenly comes up with the answer, we say they have reached a solution by a flash of "insight." Insight is often regarded as the highest form of learning, and a sign of intelligence. Do animals ever show the ability to solve a problem by using a purely mental process?

Chimpanzees placed in a room with a bunch of bananas hung out of reach, but with some boxes scattered on the floor, will sit and contemplate the situation. Then one may realize the answer and pile up the boxes to make a tower to reach the food. A dog, separated from its owner by a high fence, may suddenly realize that the best way of being reunited is not to try to get through or over the fence, but to take the long route around it. These could be regarded as examples of insight. Generally, however, even though the learning capacity of other animals is often surprisingly good, there is little evidence that they are capable of thinking about things in an abstract way as we humans can.

Proficient learners

▲ Gorillas have been found to need little training to perform simple tasks. They can understand some spoken words, and can learn to use symbols to make requests, describe objects, or direct the trainer's attention.

► Food is placed at the end of each of the arms of an experimental maze. The rat's task is to collect all the food in the most efficient way. To avoid visiting an arm more than once, the rat must learn to distinguish between them. It soon achieves this by relating them to landmarks in the room. The red line, made by a light strapped to the rat, traces its efficient route.

▼ The Skinner box has become a standard piece of experimental apparatus. A rat swiftly learns to press a lever on the box to get a food reward from inside.

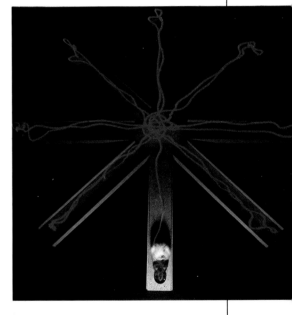

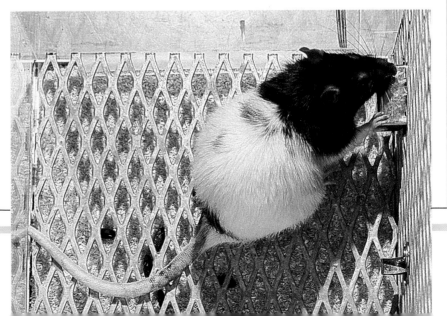

ANIMAL BUILDERS

A weaverbird bends twigs to form a loop hanging below a branch. Now he brings strips of grass and, sitting in the center, sews them into the loop and around himself to make the beginnings of a nest. With hundreds more strips, he completes an enclosed nest chamber, complete with entrance tunnel.

Many species of animal can build very impressive structures. The most skilled groups are the birds, spiders and insects, but even some of the simplest animals are able to build surprisingly well. Some tiny amoebas build intricate sand-grain cases. Just single-celled and lacking a nervous system, they pick up minute sand grains of the right size and store them inside the cell. When the cell divides, the sand grains come to the surface of the new cells and are arranged with different sized grains in different places, to give the standard shaped case for that species.

BURROWS
Some mammals are accomplished underground architects. Badgers can build setts made up of several sleeping chambers and connecting tunnels which, in an old sett, can be hundreds

▲A beaver's dam about 7ft high holds back water to form a pond. It is solidly constructed, with mud, stones, and interwoven sticks and branches.

of yards in length. Many rodents are good burrowers. Some, like the mole-rats, live an underground life most of the time, finding roots to feed on as they move through their tunnels. Moles too are well-adapted for living underground. They hunt worms in their tunnels. Both moles and mole-rats may build nest-mounds which are raised above the ground surface, but their complexity is seen only if they are dug out.

▶An underside view of the nest of a social wasp, *Polybia occidentalis*. The papery nest is made of wood fibers, which the wasps chew into a pulp.

The only mammal that makes much of a "building" above ground is the beaver. It constructs log dams which may be many yards long and up to 10ft high. These dams create lagoons in which the beaver builds a "lodge" for the family to live in.

VENTILATION ENGINEERS
Some apparently simple mammal tunnels are quite sophisticated in operation. The Black-tailed prairie

▼▶Each Ehrenberg's mole-rat makes its own system of tunnels up to 320yd long. A breeding mound contains food stores as well as a nest chamber.

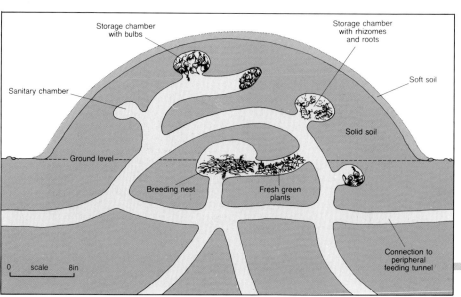

Storage chamber with bulbs

Storage chamber with rhizomes and roots

Sanitary chamber

Soft soil

Ground level

Solid soil

Breeding nest

Fresh green plants

Connection to peripheral feeding tunnel

0   scale   8in

dog makes one with a mound round the entrance to prevent flooding when it rains. But the animals show even more engineering ingenuity than that. One end of a tunnel is encircled by a low ring of earth, while the other is surrounded by a more volcano-like ring. When wind blows across the prairie the air speed is greater over the higher cone, making the pressure at that point lower than at the other end of the tunnel. Thus air is drawn through the entire system to provide very effective ventilation.

Perhaps the best nest ventilation and air conditioning, however, is achieved by the termites. Those of the African genus *Macrotermes* live in tall mound nests with outer walls 20in thick. Within these walls the termites build air-carrying channels that connect up with "cellars" excavated in the damp ground below

▼An orb-web spider sits at the center of its web waiting for an insect to blunder into the sticky threads. They are made of silk spun by the spider.

the nest. Air warmed by the insects' activities rises from the living area and fungus gardens, and then passes down the outer channels, cooling as it descends into the ground. There its humidity increases as it is circulated through the moist cellar before rising again to the living area. The nest-building behavior of all these tiny insects creates a huge structure that is more efficiently "air-conditioned" than many of the buildings that we humans live in.

INSECT NESTS
Like termites, the other social insects – the ants, bees and wasps – are also accomplished builders. The different kinds of ant show a variety of nest-building behavior. Several build below ground, like the Black garden ant. Others make a mound of earth, like the Yellow meadow ant, or a nest covered with a pile of twigs and pine needles, like the Wood ant. Some ants make their nests in trees, or even in galls that sometimes form on twigs.

Wasp and bee nests are notable for the arrangement of cells in the comb that the workers build. Each cell is six-sided, an arrangement which is strong and allows the maximum number to be packed into the available space. But the animals have no knowledge of geometry – they build this way purely by instinct. Wasp nests are made of a papery substance, produced by chewing up plant fibers. Bees make their nests using wax secreted by the bees themselves to construct the intricate comb.

COCOONS
Except for the social groups the only other "builders" among the insects are the butterflies, moths and caddisflies, all of which can secrete silk. Caddisfly larvae use silk as a cement to hold sand grains and fragments of plants together in the form of a protective case around the animal's body. Silk can also be used on its own to make a cocoon in which to pupate, as in some moths. The silk worm is a moth

▲The Penduline tit builds a hanging nest shaped like a purse. Although it is made of delicate materials, these are skillfully woven together to give a very strong structure which has a felt-like texture.

▼To build its domed nest, the Rufous hornero uses up to 2,500 pellets of clay, strengthened with hairs and other fibers. A narrow entrance leads to a grass-lined chamber about 8in across.

caterpillar that is farmed in the Far East because of its ability to spin a cocoon made of high quality silk. The silk strands are unwound from the cocoons by machine and woven into expensive fabrics.

WEBS

Another important group of animals – the spiders – also use silk as a building material. Some secrete a silk thread to act merely as a safety drag line or a parachute, but many spiders spin complicated webs which act as traps for insects. The purse-web spider lives in a burrow, above which it spins a finger-like silk sleeve. When prey walks over this, the spider rushes up and bites it through the silk, before pulling it into its lair.

The best-known type of web, however, is the orb-web. This is built to a fixed plan typical of the particular species. Radial threads are made first, then the spider travels round these in a spiral, making the sticky silk net which will trap insects.

BIRDS' NESTS

Though some make no nest, birds as a group do build an incredible variety of structures in which to lay their eggs. They may be little more than a pile of sticks, as in crows or some eagles. They can be made of mud, or can include fur, feathers and plants in their construction. Some, such as the nests of hummingbirds, which are built of lichens, down and spider silk, are amazingly small and delicate. The basic ability to build these nests is part of each bird's instinctive behavior, though they do seem to get better at construction with practice.

Weaverbirds make some of the most complex nests. They are roofed, hanging basketwork structures, made from strips of grass and palm leaves. Weaverbirds are able to make a variety of loops and stitches to hold their nests together. They really sew with their beak rather than weave.

SLEEP AND OTHER RHYTHMS

It is ten minutes after sunset. A bat emerges from the eaves of a house and flies off into the night. Then, faster and faster, more bats leave the roost. After a while all have gone. But before dawn all the bats return. They find nooks among the roof timbers, hang head downwards, and settle for a good day's sleep.

Almost all animals live in an environment in which some of the events that affect their lives are rhythmic. Night and day, the tides, the phases of the Moon, the seasons of the year – all these can have effects on behavior.

DAILY RHYTHMS

Animals have strong internal rhythms that keep their bodies in step with their surroundings. Humans have a daily cycle of changes in body temperature and alertness. Other animals have their "internal clocks" too. They are important to all creatures but can perhaps be seen most readily in our pets. A dog will turn up for its meal at the exact time every day without being able to read a watch.

Many vertebrates spend part of every day sleeping, and these periods are usually closely synchronized with the intervals of darkness or light.

IN STEP WITH THE MOON

Some animal rhythms are in phase with the Moon. The Moon influences the height of tides, and many aquatic organisms, including some fishes and also invertebrates such as king crabs, time their spawning to coincide with the highest tides. Even for annual breeders the Moon may be important. The marine Palolo worm forms vast mating swarms during the last quarter Moon in October and November.

ANNUAL RHYTHMS

Animals characteristically breed at a certain optimum time of year in temperate regions, usually in the spring or summer. In both birds and mammals the increase in day length at this time of year is often the stimulus that brings them into breeding condition. Some, such as ptarmigans and stoats, also change the color of their coat in response to the annual cycle. In many birds, and some mammals the urge to migrate is governed by an annual rhythm.

TORPOR AND HIBERNATION

When some animals sleep their body temperature falls and all body processes slow down. This is a special kind of sleep known as torpor. Hummingbirds become torpid at night, thereby saving energy. Insect-eating bats in temperate regions have the opposite rhythm, becoming torpid during the day.

A seasonal – winter – rhythm of torpor and wakefulness is known as hibernation. Many animals, such as hedgehogs, spend much of the winter in this state. During such hibernation, with a body temperature only a little above the surroundings, a small mammal needs only one seventeenth of the energy it would have used had it remained active. But it does need some body fat – its energy store – left at the end of hibernation to burn up to raise itself to normal operating temperature. A small mammal like a bat may be able to warm itself up in about half an hour. A larger one such as a marmot may take many hours.

Hibernation is a way of surviving periods of food scarcity but some animals become seasonally torpid to avoid the worst conditions in desert regions. This is called estivation.

▲Spawning grunions deposit eggs high
on the beach during spring tides when
the Moon is full. Hatchling grunions swim
off at the next spring tide.

▶This hibernating Daubenton's bat is
covered with dew. Its body temperature
has dropped to that of its surroundings
in a cold, damp cave.

▼Penguins in vast numbers exploit the
abundance of krill in the Antarctic
summer. Their internal clock tells these
Adelie penguins when to head north to
their breeding grounds before winter.

ANIMAL CULTURE

Two young Snow geese are on their first migration. They fly with their parents south from their nesting grounds in Canada to winter in Texas. In the spring they return with their parents to the north. Now they have been shown the "right" nesting region the young birds will be able to find their way to it next year. They belong to a group with a particular cultural identity.

For humans, culture means many things. In different parts of the world people wear different clothes, use different feeding utensils, eat different food, have different patterns of tools, and so on. They also have different customs concerning matters like marriage and how families are run. Thus, though there are typical ways for humans to behave, there are also differences between groups. These derive from the customs, lore and knowledge handed down through generations. In humans, a particular cultural group might be recognized as one whose behavioral habits characteristically differ from those of any other.

SHARED BEHAVIOR

The culture of a group is passed on by example and imitation. It is not inherited as an instinct. Just as in humans, other animals can show cultural differences between groups within the same species. The passing of information between animals by behavioral methods results in the spread of a particular culture.

Whereas inherited factors can be passed on only from parent to offspring, behavior learned by one animal from another can pass to any member of the group. The spread of a particular form of behavior through a population by imitation can be very fast.

LEARNING CAPACITY

For information to pass from one individual to another by imitation or "teaching," the species has to possess the ability to learn. Most examples of culture change in animals have therefore been noticed in those which have a large brain – birds and mammals. But it is possible for some lower animals to pass on behavioral information. The dances of a scout honeybee returning to the colony convey with remarkable accuracy the type of food the bee found and its distance and direction from the hive. The other workers register the message and act on it. If the scout bee reports good heather flowers, a "heather flower culture" spreads throughout the hive. Later, the attention of the colony may be turned to another crop and the culture of the hive will change.

TAMENESS AND WILDNESS

Where predators are few, as on islands, animals can be very tame and unwary. Humans are apt to be predators of the worst sort on island species, and may bring about a change in their behavior. A visitor to the Galapagos Islands in 1684 could write, "Turtle doves were so tame, that they would often alight on our hats and arms, so that we could take them alive: they are not fearing man, until such time as some of our company did fire at them, whereby they were rendered more shy."

Such shyness can be a cultural trait, passed from one animal to another relatively rapidly. If one or two badgers in a sett have an alarming experience the whole family group may become more wary. It is not

▶ A diver and Bottle-nosed dolphin greet one another underwater. Animals such as monkeys, apes and dolphins can solve problems by reasoning and can learn to discriminate between objects, patterns and colors. They also interact with one another socially using language, as we do.

necessary for every animal in the group to be frightened individually – each takes its cue from another. Foxes and otters are both largely nocturnal animals, but in those remote parts of Britain where they are undisturbed they may also be active during the day. Thus there can be cultural differences between the way groups in different areas behave.

PASSING ON NEW IDEAS

Two of the most famous instances of the emergence of a different culture in a group of animals are interesting because they involved passing on a "new invention." One of these was the discovery by a young female macaque in an isolated experimental colony living by the sea in Japan that food could be improved by washing it. She found she could remove sand from sweet potatoes, and also from grains of rice. When the rice was thrown in the water sand-free grains could be skimmed off the surface. It was not long before other macaques in the group started copying this technique and found the results to their liking. The behavior is now widespread throughout the colony.

In another case, an English Blue tit discovered, by accident, that the cream on top of a bottle of milk (milk is delivered to the door in bottles in England) was a good food, and that it could break into the foil top of the bottle. Though this occurred at just a single location, the technique spread until Blue tits all over Britain seemed to know that they could get an easy meal in this manner.

▲ Smaller birds mobbing a kookaburra. Mobbing behavior against predators is believed to be a type of behavior that can spread culturally.

Japanese macaques washing sweet potatoes in the sea. Washing these vegetables removes sand, and may add a pleasant saltiness. The technique was discovered by a young female called Imo, but it was soon copied and spread throughout the whole troop. At first only Imo's immediate companions imitated her. After 4 months her mother started washing food and then the habit spread rapidly.

TERMITES FOR TEA

There are many examples of young animals learning from their elders how to get at a particular food item. To twirl a stick or grass stem down the hole of a termite nest, and then lick off the insects that stick to it, is a difficult skill for a young chimpanzee to master. But young animals will watch carefully as older animals perform the task, and by persistent imitation they eventually acquire the skill (see page 78). Oystercatchers have two main sources of food: ready-to-eat marine worms, or mussels which are difficult to extract. Some groups feed on one, others on the other. A chick in the "worm culture" group stays with its parents for only about 6 or 7 weeks. In the "mussel culture" group, on the other hand, a chick may remain dependent on its parents for up to 26 weeks because it takes much longer to learn the difficult technique of getting the flesh out of the mussel shell.

CULTURAL SONGS

Cultural groups consisting of only two individuals are formed by some species of small finch. Each member of a breeding pair learns its call structure from the other, with the result that their calls are the same. They are, however, slightly different from those of any other pair. This will obviously help mated individuals to recognize one another. In other cases a whole population can have its own culturally transmitted song "dialect."

It has been thought that dialects are a way of keeping populations separate and preventing interbreeding. In many species this is probably correct but in at least one the opposite seems to be the case. The male saddleback, a rare New Zealand bird about the size of a blackbird, learns its song, not as a fledgling but after it has dispersed from the place where it was hatched. It moves to an area where the birds have a different dialect to that of its father. It then learns this version of the song, joining a new culture. In this manner reproductive mixing of the populations seems to be ensured.

Observers have noticed that a young male sometimes makes a slight error in learning. His "defective" song may be copied by others, and a new song sweeps through the population.

▲ Elephants in the Addo Park in South Africa were hunted, one by one, in 1919. A few survived, becoming very wary and dangerous. No shooting has taken place for 50 years, but the present herd has kept the culture of wary behavior.

CULTURAL ADVANTAGES

What are the advantages of changing behavior by cultural imitation? The obvious one is that this type of change can move swiftly through a population. You have only to think of how "crazes" for roller-skating, playing with yo-yos, and so on can spread very rapidly through a human population. If animals had to rely on inheritance to introduce and then fix a behavioral change in a population it would take very many generations, but a cultural change can take place in just one.

Provided that a species has the mental capacity to learn from the example of others, a chance piece of behavior that seems to be of some benefit can be rapidly consolidated. The success of the human species in such a relatively short time – but perhaps its weaknesses too – probably owes much to this mechanism.

GLOSSARY

Adult A fully developed animal that is mature and capable of breeding.

Aestivation (also **estivation**) A state of **dormancy** during the summer. Mainly undertaken by some species living in inhospitably hot, dry regions.

Aggression Behavior that involves attacking or threatening another animal.

Appeasement Behavior that stops another animal carrying through an attack. It is often the opposite of **threat** behavior. For example, a gull shows its beak in threat, but hides it in appeasement.

Behavior Any of an animal's actions, rather than its structure.

Camouflage Colors, patterns and associated behavior of animals that allow them to blend with their surroundings and remain undetected by **predators**.

Carnivore An animal that feeds on other animals.

Caste Those members of a social species that are adapted, by their structure and behavior, to perform a particular task, such as worker bees.

Commensalism An association between two species such that one of them benefits without appreciable cost to the other.

Contact call A sound made by an animal that helps it to keep in touch with its partner or other members of its group.

Cooperation The assistance of one animal by another where both gain. For example, many watching eyes make it easier for herd animals to spot **predators**.

Cultural evolution Changes in behavior that spread through a population by imitation and learning, without genetic change being involved in creating them.

Culture A set of patterns of behavior that are reproduced by learning. They are often passed from generation to generation.

Displacement activity Seemingly irrelevant behavior produced by an animal at times when there is conflict between two things it might do, such as fighting or fleeing.

Display A pattern of things done by one animal that gives information to other animals. It may be seen or heard. Greeting, threatening or courtship may involve displays between animals.

Distraction display A **display** in which, for example, a mother bird leads a **predator** away from her defenseless young.

Dominance The ability of an animal to take precedence over another for food, mates or good resting positions. Dominance may be, but is not necessarily, achieved by fighting.

Dormancy A state of deep sleep in which all body processes slow down to reduce energy consumption so that an animal can survive for long periods without feeding.

Echolocation Finding the position of objects by sending out a high-pitched sound and listening to its echoes.

Ethology The scientific study of natural animal behavior.

Filter-feeding A method of obtaining food by straining small particles from the water.

Habitat The surroundings in which an animal lives, including the plant life, other animals, the physical landscape and climate.

Habituation A kind of simple learning in which an animal stops responding to something that happens repeatedly in its surroundings.

Harem A group of females guarded by a single male that mates with them and keeps other males away.

Herbivore An animal that eats plants.

Hibernation A state of **dormancy** in winter. In mammals it may involve cooling of the body and slowing of the body processes such as breathing.

Hierarchy The order into which a group of animals sorts itself, with some dominant to others. *See* **dominance**.

Hoarding Hiding food away in a store or cache to which the animal later returns.

Home range The area within which an individual animal usually lives.

Homing Returning to a place accurately from a distance after moving, or being moved, away.

Imprinting The process by which young animals respond to and learn the features of an object to follow (usually their parent) early in life.

Insight A type of learning which involves the ability to recognize the relationship between objects in order to "solve" a problem mentally.

Instinct Behavior that is built into an animal; that portion of behavior which is inherited rather than learned.

Intelligence The capacity that enables an individual to learn tasks, reason and solve problems.

Language Strictly, communication between people using words. But often used to describe all kinds of animal communication.

Lek A communal mating ground used for displays.

Migration Long-distance journeys made by animals, particularly regular seasonal movements, as between nesting and wintering grounds.

Mimicry (1) Resemblance in shape, color or pattern between two animals, that may give one or both an advantage. For example some harmless flies mimic wasps. (2) Imitation of behavior, as when one bird mimics the song of another.

Mobbing Surrounding and noisily confronting a **predator** in a collective attempt to drive it away. Many kinds of small bird will join in mobbing a hawk or owl.

Mouthbrooding A kind of parental care seen in some fishes, in which the female protects the eggs inside her mouth until they hatch.

Navigation The ability to find the way to a specific site from another distant position.

Omnivore An animal that eats both animal and plant material.

Orientation The ability to take up a particular direction when moving through the environment; for example, setting a course at a particular angle relative to the Sun.

Parasitism One species living on or inside another one, feeding at the host's expense.

Pheromone An air-borne chemical (smell) produced by an animal that can be detected in minute quantities by another. It acts as a signal and produces a reaction in the receiving animal. Commonly used as an attractant between the sexes.

Population A separate group of animals of the same species, as for example, in a particular geographical area. Physical barriers usually prevent different populations from mixing.

Predator An animal that hunts other live animals as its prey.

Reflex An automatic response made by an animal to something in its surroundings, such as the pupil of the eye contracting in bright light.

Regurgitation Bringing food up from the stomach or crop to feed the young, as in wolves, bees and many species of bird.

Rutting The special behavior of male animals that occurs during the breeding season. Used particularly of deer and antelopes.

Scavenger An animal that eats dead animals and plants, perhaps including decaying matter.

Scent-marking The labeling of objects or individuals with scent, either from special glands or in the urine or feces. Scent marks act as signals to other animals.

Spawning The production of eggs and sperm by species in which these are released into the water and fertilization is external (outside the female's body).

Species The division of animal classification below genus; a group of animals of the same structure that can breed together.

Stereotyped Describes a fixed and constant behavior pattern, particularly one that is much repeated, such as the monotonous pacing of some caged animals.

Strategy The mode of behavior used by an animal when it could, either in theory or practice, have a choice of more than one way to react to a situation.

Stress A state produced in an animal by pain, discomfort, overcrowding or other adverse factors. Mild stress may lead to changes in the animal's behavior which enable it to cope. Extreme stress, on the other hand, may be lethal.

Stridulation A method of sound production in which two parts of the body, such as a leg and a wing, are scraped together; the chirping song of grasshopers is an example.

Symbiosis An association between two species in which both gain some form of benefit.

Territory The area in which an animal or group of animals lives and which it defends against intruders.

Threat Behavior that signals to another animal that the first is going to, or might, attack.

Torpor A state of deep sleep similar to **dormancy**.

Tradition Behavior shared by individuals in a population and passed from one generation to the next by learning.

Trial and error A form of learning in which an animal learns that a certain type of behavior brings a certain consequence. At first the behavior may be chance, but if it brings a benefit the animal will repeat it.

INDEX

93

FURTHER READING

Alcock, J. (1984), *Animal Behavior: An Evolutionary Approach* (3rd edn), Sinauer, Sunderland, Massachusetts

Barnard, C. J. (1983), *Animal Behaviour: Ecology and Evolution*, Croom Helm, London

Boakes, R. A. (1984), *From Darwin to Behaviourism: Psychology and the Minds of Animals*, Cambridge University Press, Cambridge.

Bonner, J. T. (1980), *The Evolution of Culture in Animals*, Princeton University Press, Princeton.

Brian, M. V. (1983), *Social Insects: Ecology and Behavioural Biology*, Chapman & Hall, London.

Broom, D. M. (1981), *Biology of Behaviour*, Cambridge University Press, Cambridge.

Brown, J. L. (1975), *The Evolution of Behavior*, Norton, New York.

Daly, M and Wilson, M. (1983), *Sex Evolution and Behavior* (2nd edn), Willard Grant, Boston.

Dawkins, R. (1978), *The Selfish Gene*, Oxford University Press, Oxford.

Dewsbury, D. A. (1978), *Comparative Animal Behavior*, McGraw-Hill, New York.

Frisch, K. von (1966), *The Dancing Bees*, Methuen, London

Gould, J. L. (1982), *Ethology*, Norton, New York.

Halliday, T. R. (1980), *Sexual Strategy*. Oxford University Press, Oxford.

Halliday, T. R. and Slater, P. J. B. (1983), *Animal Behaviour*, vols I-III, Blackwell Scientific Publications, Oxford.

Heinrich, B. (1979), *Bumblebee Economics*, Harvard University Press, Cambridge, Massachusetts.

Hinde, R. A. (1970), *Animal Behaviour*, McGraw-Hill, New York.

Hinde, R. A. (1982), *Ethology*, Oxford University Press, Oxford.

Krebs, J. R. and Davies, N. B. (1981), *An Introduction to Behavioural Ecology*, Blackwell Scientific Publications, Oxford.

Lea, S. E. G. (1984), *Instinct, Environment and Behaviour*, Methuen, London and New York.

Lorenz K. Z. (1952), *King Solomon's Ring*, Methuen, London and Crowell, New York.

McFarland, D. J. (ed) (1981), *The Oxford Companion to Animal Behaviour*, Oxford University Press, Oxford.

Marler, P, and Hamilton, W. J. III (1966), *Mechanisms of Animal Behaviour*, Wiley, New York and London.

Owen, D. (1980), *Camouflage and Mimicry*. Oxxford University Press, Oxford

Schmidt-Koenig, K. (1979), *Avian Orientation and Navigation*, Academic Press, London and New York.

Sebeok, T. A. (ed) (1977), *How Animals Communicate*, Indiana University Press, Bloomington.

Slater, P. J. B. (ed) (1986), *The Encyclopedia of Animal Behavior*, Fact on File, New York.

Smith, W. J. (1977), *The Behavior of Communicating*, Harvard University Press, Cambridge, Massachusetts.

Tinbergen, N. (1958), *Curious Naturalists*, Country Life, London and Doubleday, New York.

Trivers, R. (1985), *Social Evolution*, Benjamin/Cummings, Menlo Park, California.

Wickler, W. (1968), *Mimicry in Plants and Animals*, Weldenfeld & Nicolson. London.

Wilson, E. O. (1971), *The Insect Societies*, Belknap Press, Harvard.

Wilson, E. O. (1975), *Sociobiology: The New Synthesis*, Belknap Press, Harvard.

Wittenberger, J. F. (1981), *Animal Social Behavior*, Duxbury Press, Boston.

ACKNOWLEDGMENTS

Picture credits

Key: t top, b bottom, c center, l left, r right.
Abbreviations: AN Agence Nature, ANT Australian Nature Transparencies, BCL Bruce Coleman Ltd, NHPA Natural History Photographic Agency, OSF Oxford Scientific Films. P. Premaphotos. PEP Planet Earth Pictures. SAL Survival Anglia Ltd. SPL Science Photo Library.

4 PEP. 6t M. Fodgen. 6b Associated Press. 7t Dwight R. Kuhn. 7b Simon Driver. 8t SAL/D. Plage. 8bl,r Priscilla Barrett. 9 Natural Imagery, William Ervin. 10 BCL/J.D. Bartlett. 11t Swift Picture Library/M. Read. 11b Simon Driver. 12-13 Richard Lewington. 14-15 PEP/P. Scoones. 16 AN. 16-17 Denys Ovenden. 19 P. 20-21 OSF/M. Fogden. 22c Priscilla Barrett. 22b,23 Denys Ovenden. 24t Priscilla Barrett. 24b Simon Driver. 25 PEP/J. Scott. 26t Denys Ovenden. 26b BCL/M. Fogden. 27 R.W. van Devender. 28t Frithfoto. 28b Priscilla Barrett. 29 Ian Willis. 30l OSF/A. Shay. 30r Premaphotos Wildlife/K. Preston Mafham. 31 M. Fogden. 32 SAL/J. Root. 33cr Simon Driver. 33b SAL/J. Bennett. 34cr Simon Driver. 34b Ian Willis. 35t BCL/J. Foott. 35c Ian Willis. 35bl Simon Driver. 35br Biofotos/Heather Angel. 36 Susan Griggs/J. Blair. 37t Mick Loates. 37b, 38t Simon Driver. 38b NHPA/P. Johnson. 39t Hayward Art Group. 39b SAL/C. Buxton & A. Price. 40 NHPA/A. Bannister. 40-41 Jacana. 42 Priscilla Barrett. 43t PEP. 43b PEP/K. Lucas.

44 Ian Willis. 45t,c Simon Driver. 45b NHPA/A. Bannister. 45 inset J. C. Dickens. 46 PEP/E. Neal. 46-47 Priscilla Barrett. 48t G. Frame. 48b Robert Gillmor. 49b Premaphotos Wildlife/K.G. Preston-Mafham. 50 BCL. 51t N. Bonner. 51b Priscilla Barrett. 52-53 Nature Photographers. 53 Dwight R. Kuhn. 54-55 Denys Ovenden. 56t BCL/Charlie Ott. 56b, 57 Robert Gillmor. 58 NHPA/Peter Johnson. 59 David Dennis. 60cl Simon Driver. 60bl Richard Lewington. 60br William Ervin. 61 Ardea. 62t PEP. 62b Robert Gillmor. 63 NHPA. 64 Ardea. 64-65 .66 Priscilla Barrett. 67 P. Veit. 68l NHPA/S. Dalton. 68r Jacana. 69t PEP. 69b Priscilla Barrett. 70. PEP/P. Scoones. 70-71, 71t Priscilla Barrett. 71cr Frans Lanting. 72t SAL/J. van Gruisen. 72b Premaphotos Wildlife/K. Preston-Mafham. 73bl. OSF/D. Macdonald. 73r Priscilla Barrett. 74cr Eric and David Hosking. 74b Robert Gillmor. 75t Ann Cumbers. 75b PEP. 76 NHPA. 77t NHPA/J. Shaw. 77b Simon Driver. 78t BCL/P. Davey. 78b OSF/R. Blythe. 79t The Gorilla Foundation/Ronald Cohn. 79c,79b T. Roper. 80t J. Kaufmann. 80bl Priscilla Barrett. 80br Simon Driver. 81 Premaphotos Wildlife/K. Preston Mafham. 82 P. Hillyard. 83t BCL. 83b NHPA. 84–85 ANT/A. Jackson. 85tl BCL. 85r Ardea. 86-87 PEP/A. Mounter. 88t SAL/D. Bartlett. 88bl BCL. 88br Orion Press. 89 Agence Nature/H. Chaumeton.

Artwork © Priscilla Barrett 1986